ONE-MINUTE TIPS FOR IMPROVING YOUR IMAGE

by Carol Brockway

Harbour House Publishers of Fine Books

Melbourne, Florida

Dedication: To my husband who has always encouraged me to believe in myself.

ONE-MINUTE TIPS FOR IMPROVING YOUR IMAGE

ISBN 0-926557-47-5

Harbor House Publishers, P.O. Box 36-0122, Melbourne, FL 32936

Coverdesign by Richard Nakamoto • Editorial work and typographical design by Publications Technologies, Eau Gallie, Florida

Printed in the United States of America

ONE-MINUTE TIPS FOR IMPROVING YOUR IMAGE

A **Harbor House book** by Carol Brockway

HERE'S A REMARKABLE BOOK FILLED WITH QUICK, EASY TIPS on everything from organizing your wardrobe to picking the right shoes — and finding your special colors.

Written in a familiar, friendly style, these hundreds of tidbits are packed with originality and good sense. The author's solid experience will help you know how to dress for the right occasions ... and present yourself with confidence!

Spend your spare minutes with these quick answers! Let's build a new and better you! An excellent gift item for the self-assured or the under-confident! Renovate your life — and be surprised! Stimulate your personal creativity as the author helps you accept what is OK ... or understand what you need to do today!

SHE SPEAKS FROM EXPERIENCE — Carol Brockway is the longtime hostess of the *Improving Your Image* radio program and has long been one of the top ten teachers of the Image of Loveliness programs founded by author Joanne Wallace, founder of the Image Improvement seminars and courses.

What an invaluable reference she brings to your fingertips — with sections on such a range of topics as:

Come, improve your image ... as you enjoy these marvelous tidbits!

Other fine titles from the Publisher:

Nicky Cruz

Devil on the Run
"Brothers & Sisters, We Have a Problem
Destined to Win
How to Fight Back

David Wilkerson

A Final Warning to America — compiled and edited by Nicky Cruz

Keith Wilkerson

Midnight Raiders
Nightlark, Runner
Twilight Rebels

Dan Wooding

Miracles in Sin City (with Howard Cooper)
Singing in the Dark (with Barry Taylor)

Dr. Robert Schuller & Dr. Paul Yonggi Cho

Expand Your Horizon: (How to Make Your Faith Work!) with Tommy Reid, John Meares and Richard Halverson

Reinhard Bonnke

Plundering Hell to Populate Heaven: The Vision of Reinhard Bonnke

Benson Idahosa

Faith + Works = Success

Ken Gaub

God's Got Your Number

Van Johnson with Lloyd Hildebrand

Tackle the Impossible!

David Edwards with David Hazard

The Joy of Intimacy

Contents

Introduction

This is a note to my special friends who love improving their image.

Anyone who needs more time, less stress and anxiety needs to read this book.

Over the years, I have taught many women how to improve their image and save money in the process. Sometimes putting old habits behind and creating new ones can be hard. This book is for everyone who needs a quick, easy-to-find improvement tip for everyday problems without having to read pages and pages to find a solution. These quick, easy tips are for women and men who have too much to do and need something organized for them without taking time to find it.

Today we are all expected to be groomed and put together in every aspect. This takes time and knowledge and this resource book is meant to save you time and give you tricks that will work with a minimum amount of effort.

So, relax and accept the fact that you are not a superwoman or superman. Enjoy putting some practical, easy tips into practice. The tips are short, written in simple English, easy to read and understand. We can read volumes of books, but if we do not put into practice what we already know, the knowledge gained is useless. To know how to do something and not do it is like not knowing it at all!

After two and one-half years on the radio providing easy tips for solutions to everyday problems, I decided to write this book. It can be of value to each person in solving the frustrating problems that beset us all. That's what this book is all about.

CHAPTER 1

I Corinthians 14:40
"...everything should be done in a fitting and orderly way". LB

LET'S START WITH THE CLOSET

One of the first places to start a self-image inventory is your closet.

Very few women feel theirs is adequate. But you need to be able to understand your closet before you summon a wrecking crew and carpenters to whip up something expansive and organizable — a nice, big closet that you feel good about.

What do you need to understand about your existing closet? You need to look at:

- Its organization (or lack thereof) — and
- Its contents (including stuff that could be put elsewhere, such as the the curb).

What's wrong with your closet?

You can't find anything? Then, investing in new clothes doesn't make any sense if you can't find anything anyway.

But, you say, you need to improve your look dramatically? Buying new, expensive suits and dresses is not the answer if it is already a terrible hassle to find things and put them together each day.

You need a closet system that will work for your lifestyle. So, consider what will work best for you— what will help you start feeling good about your closet.

Sometimes, dressing smartly is not a matter of new clothes or how much space you have — but instead how successful you are at using what you already have.

Messy closets are as big an energy waster as unorganized office files. Take a long, objective look at your closet. Your first response is probably that you don't have enough space! The truth is there is more space than you think.

Here are some quick tips to help you get organization back into an important part of your life. Start feeling good about your closet.

CLOSET ORGANIZATION

In order to get a good look at your closet:

- Take everything out. Do the same thing with your dresser drawers — and anywhere else you keep clothes that you see seldom. You will get a different perspective of your wardrobe. You can easily weed out unwearables or non-wearables. You will be left with a clear picture of what goes together and what you need.
- To get your closet to better serve you, put all of your blouses, skirts, sweaters, pants, shirts sweaters and jackets together. Try all the possible combinations that will work together. Then tie them together with accessories.
- I also like to divide my clothes into dresses, casual or sporty blouses, and dress blouses. This makes it easy to pull an outfit together.
- Store often-used clothes and shoes within easy reach.
- Keep all your classic styles. They are wearable year after year. For example, a jacket with the length not too long or too short or a lapel not too narrow nor too wide is considered classic. Keep it. Accessories can update these clothes and make them look fresh and new.
- Take out-of-season clothes from the closet. Store them elsewhere. It's too hard to see what you have when everything is mixed together. So, hang evening clothes and out-of-season clothes in different places than the closet you use each day.
- All the clothes that fit you 10 years ago need to be removed. Usually clothes this old are out of date. Even if you are lucky and reach your honeymoon weight again, you will want a new look.
- Be sure you have followed the closet cleaning rules before you shop. Everything that is too small, the wrong color, the wrong line or style should be removed. Put aside those that need mending. Give to charity those that no longer work for you. Your closet may look bare but you cannot see what you need nor add to your coordination if the closet is jammed full of unwearables.
- Let go of possessions from yesterday stuffed into closets, under beds, and crammed into dresser drawers. Unclutter your life.

- Some items need to be discarded not because they are old but because you know it was a mistake to buy them. Opening your closet each morning and facing old mistakes is not good. It is certainly no way to make dressing a pleasant activity.
- You might think about moving little used clothing to the back of your closet. If it has not been worn in a given length of time, get rid of it.
- If you have done your closet weeding properly, everything in your wardrobe should be something you are currently wearing or is wearable. Everything in your closet should hang without wrinkles and should be easy to pull out without tugging. Don't let those items get out of sight and out of mind and lose some good wearing times.
- The big stress remover in closet organization is to keep everything in your view so you do not have to uncover boxes to find what you are looking for.
- Use multiple clip-on hangers for skirts and blouses to conserve space.
- A closet that is organized can be fun, can relieve anxiety and stress, and be not only a good time-saver but also save wear and tear on clothing. Properly hung or correctly folded clothing will last much longer.
- Keep everything visible so searching in back of the closet and on the floor is eliminated. There is nothing more frustrating than having to hunt for something.
- Use modular shelves and basket storage systems to get maximum use of space. There are many types available which can usually be found at your local discount store.
- Put things back where they belong. Say to yourself "How will I find it next time if I don't put it back where it belongs?"
- Use multi-level rods to maximize closet space. Jackets on top and slacks on the lower level make some areas of your closet do double duty.
- Invest in sturdy, well made hangers. They help clothes keep their shape longer. They usually go on sale along with plastic see-through shoe boxes.
- Be sure storage space is clear and dry. Damp basements may provide space, but may also promote mildew damage.
- Plastic or ceramic hooks are great for hanging robes, nightgowns and bulky items. They can be put on the back of closet doors, bathroom doors or other out-of-the-way places..
- If your weight varies, remove the clothes that don't fit and make room for new clothes.
- Don't hang onto clothes unless you dearly love them, hoping for a weight goal to be reached. Chances are you will want some new clothes when you reach your goal. Keep in your closet only the clothes you really wear.
- An organized closet simplifies getting dressed and leads to an organized and happy day.
- Keep your closet in order so you can continue to add coordinated items.
- Resolve to clean your closet at least at the beginning of each new season.
- Hang a scented deodorizer in each closet and change scent frequently.
- Place the clothes most often worn in the front part of drawers. This will keep the drawer from looking like a whirlwind went through it.
- Try rolling instead of folding towels or sheets in your linen closet. This will save space and provide a neat look to the closet as well as minimizing wrinkles.

- Keep articles you most often use in drawers that are easiest to pull out.

FINDING YOUR ACCESSORIES

- Keep jewelry, lingerie and belts in special designated places. For example, all necklaces should have their own place. There are many hanging racks available to keep them from becoming tangled.
- Belts can also be put in plastic see-through boxes for easy identification. Keep a lookout for sales on this item. They can be a bit expensive but they normally go on sale about three times a year.
- Mug racks and hanging extenders are great for hanging belts and jewelry. A board with pegs or hooks will keep those necklaces and chains in order. They can be put on the back of a closet door or hung against on an out-of-the-way wall.
- A separate dresser tray for often-used jewelry or watches can be a big help. This is especially good for jewelry you wear every day.
- To keep earrings separate and easy to find, use a mechanic's multiple-drawer work bench organizer normally used for screws or small parts. This doesn't sound too glamorous but it sure does the trick. It can be stored on the shelf in your closet.
- Clear plastic shoe boxes are easy storage for shoes and you can see which shoes you want. If you do not want to spend money for clear boxes, use the box each pair came in and mark the end boldly with the proper shoe description so they can easily be identified. I have also used tape on the ends with a marker pen and it works fine.
- Get all the shoes off the pile on the floor. You could put up a narrow shelf or use see-through plastic boxes or a hanging shoe bag but get them off the floor. This not only helps your closet organization but also your temper when you can't find the second shoe.
- Store boots upright with boot trees and cover with old sheets or pillowcases to keep the dust off. This is good for cowboy boots also. They are such an expensive item that special care should be given to them.

CARE SAVES MONEY

- Don't store clothes for a long time in plastic storage bags. Discoloration may occur or mildew formation may occur in damper climates.
- Check your combinations that work well together and make sure everything is workable and wearable before you put it back in the closet. Don't hang up clothes that need mending or cleaning. Stitch up that loose hem or replace the button now! Put clothes to be mended into a box in your sewing room not hanging in the closet.
- Put clothes away only if they are clean. Some stains become permanent if not removed quickly. Besides, dirt attracts moths.
- To get the winter odor of mothballs out of your clothes before wearing, put each garment separately into the dryer with no heat and tumble for about 10 minutes.

- Prevent moth damage by putting some whole cloves into the pockets of your woolen coats or you can put them in bags with sweaters when you are storing them.
- Avoid hanging coats, jackets and shirts or dresses on wire hangers. Molded or padded hangers maintain clothing shapes best.
- If you have a pleated skirt, paper clip the pleats together to make pressing a breeze.
- Close zippers, buttons, snaps and hooks to keep clothes hanging even. Clothes don't get the bulges, look better in your closet and they don't wrinkle as easy.
- Neatly fold all knits and fragile material like lace or beaded tops or anything that may stretch if hung. It is best to store these items in a tissue paper lined box or in drawers or on shelves.
- Stuff shoes with tissue paper to help maintain shape. Remember to take the paper out before inserting foot.
- Do not store furs in plastic bags. They need to 'breathe'. Instead wrap them in sheets and hang in a closet if you have room. If not, store them with a reliable furrier.
- If you are storing clothes that won't be used all summer, open the door occasionally and let fresh air in.

CHAPTER 2

Proverbs 31:17-18
"She is energetic, a hard worker, and watches for bargains." LB

LET'S GO SHOPPING

Now that you have your closet in order you are ready to add to your wardrobe with some intelligent good buys. I find in my own life the more knowledge that I have about a matter the better steward I am regarding spending my hard earned money.

I have watched both men and women in stores debating over purchases when they have little knowledge about what is best for them in line, proportion, or color.

Therefore, a bad purchase is made and generally sits in a closet without much wear. I do not know whether you are on a budget when shopping for clothes, but most of us need some guidelines when shopping to insure the most practical purchase.

It is always amazing to me how many people go to town to shop and have no idea what they want or how they are going to fit it into their wardrobe. When this happens the closet ends up as a mixture of clothes many times bought on impulse.

That can be very costly to the pocketbook unless there is some forethought given to what is already in our wardrobes and where we are heading in coordination.

Many clothes end up not worn and making us wonder why in the world we bought it.

Knowledge is money.

START WITH THE HANDBAG

- Choose a neutral color that will blend with many pairs of shoes in your closet.
- Nothing can downgrade a nice outfit faster than a shoddy handbag. Handbags should be of top quality and can be one of your most expensive purchases. However, in the long run it will give you many years of excellent service.
- It is better to buy an excellent bag which will cost you a little more than a mediocre one each year and not be satisfied.
- Bags and shoes do not have to match exactly but they should be in blendable or complimentary tones.
- Buy leather handbags. The vinyl ones do not last very long and will not give you your full moneys worth. One exception might be if you have an odd color outfit and you would not be using the vinyl bag frequently but only as a coordination piece. However, your everyday and frequently used bags need to be leather. Leather improves as it gets older and will last much longer as well as look much better. I have had a leather bag that looks like new and is now almost 8 years old and I use it every day.
- Be sure that the handbag has a good zipper.
- Test a handbag before you buy it. Ask your self if it will hold all you need to carry all day and does it have compartments to make your life easier. There is nothing worse than the moment you leave home you find your compact or glasses won't fit in the handbag you have chosen for the day or the bag causes you to lose everything at the bottom.
- Does the bag feel comfortable on your shoulder?
- Can you see in it easily and are frequently needed things such as keys in a convenient place?. Be aware also that some key rings will scratch things in your bag.
- One good tip for keys to be kept handy is to put them into a brightly colored eyeglass case. Even though you have a special place for them in the bag sometimes we get in a hurry and forget but when a case is used it helps to keep them handy.
- A spare eyeglass case also makes a great holder for a small hairbrush and comb.
- Another good tip is to use an eyeglass case as a holder for pens and pencils which can make pen marks on your wallet and inside the lining of the handbag.
- Look for a handbag with gussets that expand.
- Be sure that you do not over fill shoulder bags so that you pull yourself out of good body alignment for this will case many back aches.
- Keep in mind that when you change to an evening look, you need to change to a handbag that is smaller and less cluttered. A small clutch would be a good investment.
- Do not stuff evening bags so full that they bulge. It takes away from the elegant look you want to create for evening.
- For the evening carry only the essentials like a handkerchief, some small change and some keys.

- Do not carry a short strap bag like a suitcase but put through the arm and place in front of the body.
- Clutch bags are carried high up under the arm with most of the bag forward. The profile of the hand should hold the bag firmly in the front.
- Think proportion in buying a handbag. Small women carry small bags, medium women carry medium handbags etc.
- Organize your wallet and keep large bills from the small ones so you do not mistake a $10 for a $1.

SHOPPING TIPS

- Know your figure well before you shop. Do this by measuring your proportions and keeping in mind your problem areas such as where you are thick or heavy, long and short.
- Know your best colors.
- Wear comfortable clothes to shop and ones that are easy to slip on and off in the dressing room.
- Bring stockings and heels if you do not want to wear them so you can see what the outfit really will look like. It is hard to buy a dressy dress in knee socks.
- Never go shopping when you are tired or in a hurry because this is when you will make your biggest buying mistakes.
- Buying on impulse can cause some shopping errors.
- If you see something that you like in the store and you know that a sale is going to be coming soon, try the garment on when it is not on sale to get the proper size and style so that on sale day you can just go in and purchase the outfit with out trying it on in crowds.
- Get to know a favorite sales person who can guide you and help you to keep from making a purchase mistake.
- To get a good idea of your wardrobe needs, ask yourself some questions before your purchases such as how do I appear to others? How do I wish to appear?
- When you begin to buy new clothes assess your wardrobe first to see what will fit in with what you already have.
- Learn to recognize brand names and quality clothes before you buy. Better quality clothing will hang better and wear longer.
- Do not buy something just because it is a bargain. No matter how little you paid for something it is no bargain unless you wear it.
- Take a clipping from the inside of a seam of an article of clothing that you are trying to match something to because there are many shades of blues or whatever color you are trying to match and this will help avoid a return trip to the store. Time is valuable also.
- Always check the construction of the garment, such as the width of the hem, seams, buttons, button holes, and sewing construction.

- To get the best fit, always try the garment on before purchasing and study yourself in the mirror both front and back. Sometimes we forget to check the look from the backside.
- Steer clear of trendy colors, fabrics and styles unless you have a large wardrobe budget or if that is your personality. They will not stay in style very long and will date your fashion.
- When shopping it is best to buy quality in shoes, handbags, coats, suits and items that you will be wearing many times. Accessories then can cost a little less as well as lingerie, hosiery and perhaps some bargain blouses and sweaters.
- Do not let the clerk talk you into something that is not right for you. In order to do that you have to know your own figure and line and then you will know what is right and what is not right for you.
- If the store will let you take clothing home on approval this is a good way for you to work it through your wardrobe before you buy it. If I cannot move an article of clothing through at least 4 to 6 items that I have in my wardrobe already then it is probably not a very good purchase. For instance a sweater or blouse should be able to be worn with various slacks, skirts, suits, etc. Color plays an important part in being able to coordinate throughout your wardrobe.
- When you shop, have in mind what you are looking for in line, style, and color so that you do not make poor purchases and you will help extend your wardrobe rather than just add to it.
- The springtime is a good time of year to consider a suit or coat purchase.
- Other questions to ask yourself before a purchase. Will it fit easily into my wardrobe? Is it my personality? Is it financially feasible? Will it work into my lifestyle? There are no bargains if they do not work for you.
- Remember when purchasing, cleaning costs can add 100 percent or more to the cost of the garment.

Before you buy anything get the latest fashion pattern magazine and do not just look at the pictures but study it. Check the new colors, what accessories are being worn with various outfits, the type of shoe and heel, the length of the dresses, the width of the trousers as well as the length, the colors that are prominent and what is being worn together. You can even get a good idea of the latest hair styles and make up from some of the good top magazine pattern books.

Good purchases are ones that you wear a lot and that you can sometimes take from day into evening which would double its use and value to you. A good example would be a beautiful soft flowing floral blouse.

WHAT TO WATCH FOR WHEN SHOPPING:

- If you buy designer clothes, they are often put together in such a way that the pieces are already coordinated for you to go with other pieces in fabric, colors, etc. This makes shopping very easy. and by buying the additional pieces you are building a wardrobe with easily interchangeable looks from day to evening.

- If you are buying a suit and there are slacks to match, always buy them because one day you will want to wear the trouser look and another day the suited look and it is very hard to match color if they are not from the same selection or dye lot. There are going to be many times that you wish you would have completed the outfit.
- Buy only the pieces that will perform in your life. A perfect example would be a tweed skirt, trousers and jacket with a solid silk blouse that matches perfectly and a silk skirt that matches the blouse which could also make it a dress. This is investment shopping.
- It is important for you to know the difference between too small as in tight as opposed to snug as in a knit top which is suppose to hug your shoulders or the difference between oversized as in perfectly loose and just plain enormous.
- It is important to buy the best that you can afford. For instance two elegant cashmere sweaters in the correct colors for your wardrobe will last many seasons and will always make you feel elegantly dressed.
- Learn to anticipate your needs ahead of time and shop for these more expensive items during close out season sales because the initial price may be quite expensive.
- You need to enjoy what you are wearing. That is the whole point of dressing.
- Unless you have a large clothing budget, buy conservative shapes and tones first. They have the longest life in your wardrobe.
- Shop on off hours if you can so you do not have to fight the crowds. Perhaps you can take an early lunch if you work.
- Leave children at home because they become bored easily and fussy and may force you to make a hasty decision.
- Always start with a list and do not overbuy. When you buy too many things at once, its too easy to make a mistake and end up with things you do not really need or that you even intended on buying.
- If you have a hard time making a decision about something, then go home and sleep on it.
- If you will buy well made and versatile clothing you do not need near as many clothes.
- Be sure you find fabrics that look and feel rich.
- One good tip in getting a garment that is best for you is the principal of providing focus in your dress and direct the eye to where you want it to go.
- If a certain shape works good for you do not be afraid to buy a lot of it.
- Purchases should be classic enough to go from season to season. This goes for shoes also. When you find a shoe that lasts and is a shape that works for you, then buy several in different colors..
- Know when to alter something and when it is not worth it. There is a difference between too small and having a garment out of proportion than needing a little retouching to make it wearable.

- One good thing to do is to take time to analyze your past mistakes in purchasing. Look at your real fashion bloopers and ask yourself why you bought them and how they got into your wardrobe in the first place.
- Fashion bloopers come from being talked into a purchase by a pushy clerk, or perhaps you had neither the time nor patience to find what you really wanted, or perhaps it is a bargain that you could not pass up.
- Shopping as a form of entertainment can be very expensive. Clothing mistakes cost money. A lot of women that I know have a closet full of clothes and nothing to wear.
- What is in your closet not what is in the stores should dictate your purchases.
- It is always good to makes lists. It helps you to get organized and putting things down on paper can prevent some shopping errors. List the good wearable clothes you have now and also the colors and then list some items that would fit in with them and expand your present wardrobe.
- Shop warm weather clothes in January and cold weather clothes in July to save money. Shop March or April for summer clothes that are new for the season before they are picked over.
- Variety in colors and patterns should be introduced into the wardrobe in the less expensive pieces.
- Don't buy fad fashions unless you have a large clothing budget. If you must buy the fad of the season do not buy more than two items or you will have a past fashion statement before you know it.
- Start with basics and neutrals such as black, navy or camel and add color as accessories.
- The more knowledge you have about your face and figure, the more money you will save.
- Shop with make up on and your hair fixed for you will be able to tell much better what a garment will look like if you look presentable.
- Shopping takes patience and persistence to find what is right for you so do not let yourself get overtired and just buy anything.
- Don't let your self be talked into a purchase. Know yourself well enough to have some self confidence in your decision.
- Shop for fabric that goes with other pieces in your wardrobe. A good polyester or wool blend and a good gabardine are all good fabrics.
- Polyester knits are not versatile pieces to pull through your wardrobe and do not give a fashionable look.
- Buy tweeds and soft plaids to extend your wardrobe with your solids.
- Buy silk to add elegance to your wardrobe as in blouses and dresses. They now have many wonderful washable silks for those who have small children.
- Do not buy clothes for you that copy another person. It is important for you to have a style that will fit your own personality. However, do not be afraid to step out in something a little more fashionable than you bought the last time. That is how you go up the fashion ladder.

- Sometimes with new trends such as a new skirt length or drastically new style, it takes time before your eyes have chance to adjust and make the fashion become acceptable to you. Think of it this way, the changing fashions add identity to each era that passes.
- One guideline for the budget conscious is to buy investment quality shoes, handbags, coats, business suits and cut corners in less obvious places such as lingerie.
- Do not shop when you are tired or depressed because you risk buying too much and making buying mistakes.
- Set up a budget and you will feel better about your purchases.
- It does not matter how well you have planned a purchase if it doesn't fit properly, it is a waste of good money. It is best to buy clothes that are a little loose rather than a little tight.
- Take someone with you that you trust to confirm your opinion on your purchase and will be honest with you on the line and style best for you.
- Look at clothes in the natural light not just store light to keep from getting peach instead of pink or other color you did not want in your wardrobe.
- Do not buy something that has to be altered too much because you will lose the shape.
- Always stand in front of a full length mirror to get an overall picture of the garment on you.
- Check for pulled seams and loose buttons.
- Know your personality when shopping and resolve that never again will you buy anything that doesn't give you that special feeling when you wear it. These are the clothes in your closet that you wear.
- Perhaps some of the newest looks for fall or spring are not your personality, so to stay in style what you do is pick some of the key seasonal looks in line and color that do suit you and your figure and use them in smaller doses. An example would be a menswear look for women may not be for you but you could use a small dose with pretty cuff links on your blouses or wear a vest. These things are a little more feminine than the harsh men's look but would keep you up to date. Another good example would be to add strands of pearls or sweater tops to a more mannish style.
- To train your eye to be more aware of lines and proportion study store windows, fashion magazines and people on the street and try to figure out why a particular outfit looks balanced or unbalanced.
- Looking your best doesn't just happen. It takes time and motivation.

INVESTMENT SHOPPING

With the dollar not able to buy as much as it used to, it is even more important to know how to investment shop.

- Investment dressing involves weighing the number of times an item can be worn versus the cost. For instance a rain coat may be a good purchase where it rains a lot but perhaps not a good investment if only worn two or three times a year in a sunny climate.

- Buying wisely means it is best to purchase blouses, skirts, and jackets that will interchange so look for versatility in style and fabrics and if you do you can create a months worth of outfits out of 9 or 10 items.
- A good purchase is a blazer jacket in a tweed or solid color to blend throughout your wardrobe.
- Two pairs of shoes in basic and neutral colors that blend with all your clothing are good purchases. Purchase one in a basic pump and one in a dressier sling back style to extend your wardrobe and pocketbook.
- If you have a low budget for wardrobe one season just add scarves and jewelry to coordinate and update looks to the season and add interest and flair.
- It is important to develop a sense of your own style by collecting pictures from magazines and catalogs that fit the image you want such as sporty, professional or feminine, etc.
- Don't limit yourself to one look and when you shop you will have a clearer picture of what you want.
- Before purchasing any more clothing, sit down and list at least three or four of your best features. Too many women only look at the things that are wrong with them so begin to look at your good points and then accent those best features. An example would be a great waistline, then belt it. If you have really pretty eyes then wear attractive earring to draw attention upward. If you have pretty hands then a beautiful bracelet or distinctive watch will draw attention to them.

THINGS TO CHECK WHEN PURCHASING CLOTHING

- Check the zipper and see that it lies flat and even. If the zipper is puckered or curling, the chances are the entire garment has been sloppily put together and will never hang right.
- A well sewn seam sometimes has two lines of stitching. If the item you are planning to buy is torn along the seam, it has either not been well made or not been inspected.
- Hems of a skirt or dress should hang evenly and the stitching should be secure.
- Be sure to check that the linings in garments fit well and do not pull the outer fabric.
- Check the fabric match in pattern, stripes or plaid. Be sure that they match along the seam lines and pockets.
- Check the seams to see that you are not going to be sitting at your sewing machine reinforcing pulled out seams.
- Keep in mind that the quality of a garment in seams etc, is more obvious in a solid colored garment.
- Another tip is to consider the fit. Too many women buy clothes for style or color without bothering to take into consideration the way they are cut or how they fit. Unless something fits well, it won't do much for you no matter what design it is or how much it costs.
- If you plan on losing some weight still buy and wear clothes that fit you at the time. It is so discouraging to never look good when dieting. Don't buy a smaller size dress

than you take as an inspiration or incentive. It may never quite fit your reduced size and you will have thrown your money away.

- Many of us have trouble finding slacks that fit properly. Make sure they fit in the hips and rise. Bend and sit in them to see if they are comfortable. Never buy slacks or any garment for that matter that are too tight and then plan to let them out.
- Be sure that you wear the proper height shoe heel when you are purchasing because this small point can make a big difference in the look of your purchase.
- No matter how stylish your outfit is, if it does not fit into your lifestyle, then you will not get maximum wear out of it.
- Being comfortable in clothes does not necessarily mean looking sloppy.
- An outfit looks better if it does not wrinkle too much and you look comfortable free from restriction of movements as you work.
- An outfit is a good buy if it requires a minimum amount of care.
- A good thing to consider before spending your hard earned money is to buy something that is in tune with who you really are because when you wear that look you will feel comfortable.
- Another thing to consider when you purchase something is ask yourself if you are wearing the garment or if it is wearing you.
- Just because some major movie star looks wonderful in a certain look doesn't mean that the look will fit your personality and achieve the same image.
- A smart thing to remember to save money in the clothes market is to be able to wear those clothes at least two to three different ways to give you more mileage for your money.
- Go for the look of quality instead of quantity because if you buy good clothes you can wear them year in and year out without wearing them out because they are well made and keep their shape. Some traditional clothes stay in fashion forever so it is more practical to spend money on garments that will stay in style at least long enough to stabilize your wardrobe.
- When you purchase clothing keep in mind the upkeep of the garment because sometimes your dry cleaning bills can run you almost as much as the garment. If you have a garment that is made out of a washable fabric with a label that says dry clean only be sure that you dry clean it.
- It is advantageous to write down the combinations that you have made because we have a tendency to forget when they are all put back in the closet. Use your list to remind you of your new discoveries and use it also as an aid when shopping.
- To avoid making the same mistake every time that you shop, before you purchase another thing think about the things in your closet that you already have. You will probably find that your favorite clothes all have a similar mood, style, or fabric. Then you ask yourself why you love these items of clothing so very much and you can then add things to your wardrobe that you are comfortable wearing.
- Make a list of clothing items that you ended up never wearing and they hung in the back of your closet. Analyze those mistakes so that you are less prone to buying unwisely again.

- Before you go shopping for the new season, go through your closet and single out the outfits you are planning to wear that year. Then make a list of the styles and colors as well as accessories that would go well with the clothes you have so that when you do go shopping you can look for the type of clothes in the colors and fabrics you have decided you need. This keeps you from buying something just because it is marked down. It is always fun to get a bargain but it is no bargain if it is not going to fit into your wardrobe and ends up never worn.
- Lay your clothes out and combine them before you haphazardly shop for things that will extend the wardrobe.
- Don't be afraid to wear accessories because that is what really pulls fashion together.
- Cheaper clothing does tend to be cut somewhat smaller so where you might wear an 8 in a higher priced garment, you may have to buy a 10 or 12 in the cheaper brand. Judge your true size by the medium priced wear because in the less expensive garments you will generally be one size larger.
- An elegantly dressed woman knows that simplicity is a dramatic fashion statement.
- Rushing around trying to buy for a special occasion can cause some of the biggest fashion purchase mistakes so plan out your purchases ahead of time.
- If you buy clothing with the thought in mind of how many times you will be able to wear it you will get more for your dollar. That is really what investment dressing is all about. It is being able to wear things in many different ways for many different occasions.
- If you purchase a real good gabardine or wool blend suit for $200 and then you wear it once a week for at least 8 months of the year for three years the cost per wearing is $2.08.
- Colors play a part in investment buying because the neutrals, beige, gray, navy, and black as well as white can be worn year round by mixing and matching and adding different colors with them for the particular season.
- Learn to pick your clothes for comfort as well as style because confident and powerful people need to look at ease in their clothes.
- When you begin to build a wardrobe you do not have to start from scratch. If you will rethink the basic organization of the clothes you already have then you can save money.
- Learn to mix the two worlds of work and non work clothes and you may find that they may go together to expand your wardrobe with different layering.
- It is easier to pull pieces together if you stay within one theme or type of fashion. Funky clothing does not pull well into a closet of classics.
- A range of white blouses probably does not sound very exciting but they are great extenders to help make possible an entire range of the wardrobe.
- Anything you can see that you need to expand your wardrobe make a note of such as a new belt and then you can create an entirely new ensemble by purchasing only a minor investment.
- If you want to save money on clothing then remember that the versatility of the garment is more important than quantity. Each piece that you purchase should be ex-

tremely flexible and make different looks when it is worn with other accessories and separates.

- To keep nylon fabrics from yellowing, add some baking soda to both the wash and rinse water.
- To keep colors in a newly purchased article of clothing from running through the fabric such as red and blue stripes running into the white stripe, rinse with vinegar in the water to set the color.

COAT PURCHASES

- When you are looking for a coat, look for a color and shape which will work with what you already own. A classic shape is an investment and you will wear it with joy year after year.
- A good basic coat for year round would be the classic trenchcoat. The general rule is simple is best in a coat purchase.
- Stay away from too much detail because it will limit what you can wear it with as well as make the look more complicated and sometimes bulky.
- Some examples of over detailing might be big fancy buttons, too many yokes and too much stitching as well as multitudes of pocket flaps with decorations or even too many buttons. Sometimes the manufacturer gives you your moneys worth by adding accessories but this is not necessarily the best look.
- The length of the coat should cover the hem of your garment by at least a half-inch. The exception being of course the three-quarter-length coat which comes to about mid thigh.
- The sleeve length is very important because too short a sleeve will make the coat look as if it is too small.
- Check the fit of the collar and shoulder to see that it hangs evenly, comfortably and straight and does not feel heavy across the shoulders. Heaviness across the shoulders can become painful after hours of wearing it and is a sign of something wrong with the fit.
- Comfort should be a number one priority in a coat. Raise your arms easily to see that you do not feel any resistance.
- Consider carefully what you will be wearing under your coat. If you wear a lot of jackets a purchase of a cape may be good for you because it fits very comfortably over suits and jackets.
- Be sure that you try your coat on with a jacket underneath if you wear a lot of jackets.
- If you wear your coat mainly over blouses, dresses or sweaters, then to not look too large, the coat should fit more like a jacket.
- The ideal lining for a raincoat is the one that will button or zip out so that you can make the coat seasonless from winter to spring.
- Buy the best that you can afford and this means the best in fabric, workmanship and fit and a coat that will give you the longest life.

- There is not one coat that will meet all of your needs from a pair of jeans to an evening look. Therefore, carefully think your purchase and buy a coat that will go further in your wardrobe.

CHAPTER 3

Psalms 37:23 LB
"The steps of a good man are directed by the Lord." LB

MEN: MAKING THE MOST OF YOUR DOLLAR WITH CLOTHING

The leisure time in a man's life is very important. The clothes he wears for leisure are a big part of keeping that image of success. Relaxing does not mean that a man's appearance has to be less than the standard that has made him successful in the first place.

A lot of business is done on the golf course, tennis court or at a dinner party.

When selecting leisure clothes, choose them on the basis of comfort, function, and to suit your personality. This type of clothing is when a man can wear the brightest most colorful apparel and can pick and choose almost endlessly these days. Patterns and fabrics run the gamut from bold to conservative.

Success is ambition and talent, experience, good judgment, dedication, skill and some luck, but the key that often opens the way for the man to show off what he can do and give him the confidence to do it is his appearance.

Each client will look the man over to see if they think he can get the job done and what he thinks of himself. You know what your qualifications and abilities are but the client has to guess and most of the time what they have to judge on is the appearance and grooming of the man.

Your appearance should reflect a strong image of self worth.

TIPS FOR MEN IN PURCHASING A SUIT, JACKET OR TROUSER

- The suit is the uniform of success in the business world and in building a wardrobe with a look of success you should choose the look that identifies you with the leaders in your field.
- Lapels on suits should be considered when purchasing a suit because too wide or too narrow a lapel can be very dating in a suit. If you deal with a reputable retailer, you can be assured that the suit he sells will be in keeping with the current trends. Be careful however that several year old suits are not being sold and get caught with an out of date look.
- Be careful of the relationship between your size and shape and the pattern on the suit as well as the fabric and color.

SHORTER MEN

- A man who is short will look best in vertical lines in both pattern and cut of the suit.
- The jackets should be a little shorter because a long jacket makes the legs appears shorter.
- A shorter man will look best in pants that are a slim cut and not cuffed.
- Shoes should blend and belts should be the same color as the pants.

HEAVIER MEN

- A heavier man should not wear bright colors or bold patterns. Small striped suits and vertical designs are good.
- Do not wear a suit coat too tight and the jackets should be slightly longer than average.
- Vertical lines in ties are important as well as dark colors and fabrics with a flatter finish.

SLIMMER AND TALLER

- A slimmer and taller body can take the plaids, checks, and a two color combination in jacket and pants.
- Coats with broad shoulders are good.
- They look good in jackets that are loose fitting at the waist. Double breasted suits are wonderful for the slim tall man.

GENERAL TIPS

- Many men let their wives just buy for them. However, I find that many more men are taking an interest in what colors are best for them and proper success dress.

- A high price tag does not always reflect quality in men's clothes but usually you get what you pay for.
- Solid color suits are the best purchase and then you can add some tweed jackets and nice soft striped shirts and ties purchasing with color coordination in mind.
- For a first purchase, a solid color vested business suit in a good wool blend would be best. Even though vests may not be worn predominantly that particular season they soon will be in fashion again and you will always have it.
- The more contrast that you have the more authority that you will give to your client, such as a navy suit and white shirt — so, if you do not want to be as intimidating and have a more friendly look, choose the more medium shade suit which is best in sales.
- A blazer in tweed or a good wool blend is appropriate for some business occasions and can be worn on all informal occasions.
- It is not the best look to mix and match suits and sports coats or wear a suit coat with sport slacks.
- Success dressing for the business man has been relaxed some and separates are becoming more acceptable such as a tweed jacket with a nice pair of slacks. Choose where you will wear this more relaxed look however. The traditional suit is still the best in most business situations.
- The navy blazer and gray trouser are always a good fashion and business look and would be a good addition to any wardrobe.

TROUSERS

- The waistline should fit comfortably and there should be enough fabric to not pull at the derriere, thighs, hips and across the lower abdomen.
- The break of the trouser or how much fabric rests on the shoe should be slightly no more than 1/2 inch.
- Select some conservative colors that will coordinate with the other major wardrobe pieces and you can put with other jackets. Gray, navy and a touch of burgundy is a good example.
- The fewer alterations that are taken makes it better because too many changes can camouflage rather than correct the problem of an ill fitting garment.
- Do not be afraid to have some alterations. However, to make the garment look tailor made, the changes should be minimal.
- Clip a small piece of fabric from the inseam of the trouser and put it on a 3x5 card. Then all you have to do when shopping is to take the card and your ties, jackets, shirts and slacks will all be the correct color match.

THINGS TO CHECK BEFORE PURCHASING

- Develop a keen eye for details in the line of the garment.
- Check the fabric closely.
- Learn to look closely at the interior of the suit jacket or sports coat and you will see the kind of construction that makes for a comfortable and nice hanging jacket.

Critiquing the interior of a suit jacket is as important as examining the outer appearance.

- Mitered corners are the sign of a well made jacket.
- The sleeves should have enough fabric to be lengthened if needed and the armhole should be cleanly finished.
- One thing to observe when critiquing the interior of a jacket are the center seam down the back. It should have one half inch of extra fabric on both sides of the seam. This seam is a folded seam and is needed for any alterations that may be needed.
- Three or four pockets inside the jacket are a sign of quality.
- It would be good to check the inside of the collar because it should be lined but the lining should not extend past the edge of the collar.
- There should not be a gap when the jacket is buttoned.
- Check to see that the jacket hangs with the natural body line.
- The best jacket sleeve length should show a little of the shirt sleeve such as 1/4 to 1/2 inches. This is a general rule.
- The correct sleeve length for a jacket measures five inches from the end of the sleeve to the tip of the thumb.
- Jackets that are made of a good quality wool will usually be a good buy.
- When trying on a new jacket, if you will raise your arms above the head, then bring them slowly down to the sides, this will settle the jacket onto the shoulders and enable you to judge a good fit. If the fabric bunches in any area, this may indicate that the collar is not laying properly. Notice the back of the jacket. Vertical wrinkles or creases indicate the jacket is too large. If it has horizontal creases, it is an indication that it is too tight.
- Diagonal lines along the back of a jacket indicate that the opposite shoulder is too low which is a common problem and can be corrected with padding.
- A vest should fit smooth and close to the body without the slightest sign of pulling or creasing.
- Invest in quality because economy is achieved by building your wardrobe with some durability and versatility in mind.
- The navy blazer is an important mainstay in a man's wardrobe.

COATS

- Take into consideration what fashion image you wish to portray before you purchase a coat or sports jacket.
- Take into consideration the climate where you live and work.
- How much business traveling you do, where you go and what type of clients you deal with the most.
- If you give some forethought to this you can then purchase perhaps only l or 2 sport coats to cover all of your needs not only for keeping warm but also for looking good.
- If your budget can handle one regular coat and one raincoat, select a coat that is in a solid color or a conservative pattern. When you do this you are less likely to be in a

position where you would have to wear a bold patterned coat with a with a distinctively patterned suit or trousers.

- Rain coats and trench coats with zip in liners are the best buy for every man's wardrobe. It offers year round protection from inclement weather and the ideal coat for travel.
- Raincoats and trenchcoats are not a substitute for the tailored coats for the man dressed for success. Most importantly choose the right coat for you and the image you want to project.
- The best business color for the successful look in a raincoat is the neutral beige.

SHOES

- Shoes are an important purchase and should always coordinate in color to the pant your are wearing.
- Shoes experts say that the weight of the body is divided between each foot with 50% on the heel, 30% on the big toe area or ball of the foot and 20% on the little toe area.
- A wide toe box with sufficient height is important for proper weight balance. A narrow toe area squeezs the toes together diminishing balance.
- A heel higher than 1 1/2 inches is too high and shifts the body weight too much onto the toe area.
- The heel should give good support to the whole foot.
- Men's shoes should be classic, flattering and well polished. White shoes are not good with suits unless you want people to look at your feet first instead of you.
- Also, do not wear white shoes or white belts for business look. White is for a sporty ensemble.
- Out of shoe polish and your shoes are a mess, then try rubbing in a small amount of hand cream and buff to a bright shine.
- Good fashion means coordinating the color and texture of your shoes and belts. For example do not wear a black belt with brown shoes or visa versa.
- If you will try linseed oil on the soles of squeaky shoes, it will help the noise.
- Shoes, belts and hats should be hung on a rack to keep looking as nice as possible.

SOCKS

- Argyles, crew socks and whites are for sport and leisure wear only.
- Small neat patterns in socks are correct for business as long as they do not clash with the color or pattern in your suit.
- If you sit down for a business meeting the look of success is not three inches of hairy calf showing, so be sure your socks are showing instead. A nice over the calf or mid calf sock is the proper length for a neat business look
- It is best to wear black socks with all dark shoes.
- If a camel or tan shoe is worn with the coordinating suit then wear camel or tan socks.

SHIRTS

- If you like a small pattern or a narrow stripe in your shirt then be sure you coordinate it in color. If a pattern is used, it is best to wear a solid tie.
- The best business shirt is white, solid color, and stripes in pale hues. Do not wear deep solid colors for a business look, such as deep burgundy, greens, etc.

TIES

- The tie should harmonize in color with the outfit and the pattern should not conflict with the pattern of the suit or sport coat.
- Some food stains will come out of ties if you will rub a little talcum powder on and leave it overnight. Then gently brush it in the morning.
- When hanging your ties always hang them without knots from a tie rack to prevent crushing them or getting them wrinkled.
- The tie is one of the most important things that a man wears because it says success or it may make a man look unsuccessful. Squiggly ties or loud ties do not give off an air of success.
- The darker the tie the more authority the man gives off, but black ties should be only worn to funerals. The exception for this is being in the evening such as a black bow tie with a tuxedo.
- Ties mean respect, show credibility, and are a fashion statement. Some ties are a decorative filling on a man's shirt and show a mark of individuality. They can become a personal identification. They provide an important finishing touch for any business or dress up wardrobe so think what image you are wanting to portray when putting on your tie.
- The right tie with the right outfit is an essential part of creating a harmonious look. The wrong tie can wreck a perfect suit and indicates that the wearer is either careless in his dress and appearance or that he just lacks good taste or perhaps he just got dressed in the dark.
- A few rules for ties include number one it should harmonize in color with the outfit and secondly the pattern in the tie should not conflict with the pattern of the suit or sport coat. If you combine a plaid suit or sport coat with a strong patterned tie, the look seldom works.
- Solid colors in ties in conservative tones are good as well as the rep stripped tie, polka dots, and small diamonds are great also. The ties with the regimental stripes are ideal for the business man and for selling. If a man can afford only one tie, then buy the striped repeat tie.
- The width of ties varies from year to year but the determining factor in the width of ties is that they should be in direct proportion to the width of suit lapels. The wide tie with a narrow lapel destroys the harmony of an outfit and the same thing applies to a narrow tie with a wide lapel.
- The bow tie is not a business mans tie.

- Never wear your tie tied in a tiny tight knot. It should be tied just firmly enough to keep it in position.
- When purchasing a tie, the silk or silk blends are best because they tie better and do not make such a large knot.
- Do not wear white ties for business.

ACCESSORIES FOR MEN

- Accessories are important for men as well as women. One basic rule for men's jewelry is the less the better. Too much jewelry or the wrong kind of jewelry can bring negative responses.
- Tie clips should be relatively expensive or at least have the expensive look. A cheap tie clip can ruin the best tie.
- Tie tacks are popular but be careful because they can make holes in your expensive ties.
- Lapel pens that are worn should be worn only if they have significance such as an honor.
- Some men can wear tasteful ID bracelets and get away with it but most of the time they are not good especially for a business look.
- Cuff links should be simple and the expensive gold or silver are the best. Do not wear gaudy cuff links.
- When choosing a belt, buy fine leather and be aware of the belt buckle. The big heavy ornate buckles are not as good as the small clean traditional buckles with squared lines. This is a rule for buckles in business because there are many larger ornate buckles in the western world.
- Money clips are a nice gift for a man and should be simple, elegant and tasteful.
- Wallets should be the finest leather and fit flat in the back pocket without a lot of bulge. The finer the leather, the better it will work for your over all presence.
- The best color for wallets is a dark rich brown or deep burgundy.
- The larger longer pocket secretary wallet that can be carried in the suit pocket is very useful for the man that wears a lot of suits.
- An attache case should be fine leather and is usually quite expensive but worth the extra money. It is a positive symbol of success regardless of what the man is carrying in it and it always lends presence to a man. The best color to purchase is the dark rich tone of brown leather or deep maroon or burgundy. Black and gray do not look as rich.
- Attache cases should be simple and functional without a lot of decoration or hardware on it.
- The handkerchief pocket squares should match or harmonize with the tie or shirt and they add a smart touch of color.
- If you own a nice pair of woolen gloves then insert wooden clothespins in the fingers to keep them from shrinking.

GENERAL TIPS

Here are some tips on what to wear to feel the most comfortable in various situations.

- What is right is determined by the occasion and location as well as the season of the year.
- An afternoon party in the fall would lend itself to a nice pair of corduroy slacks, a sport shirt or maybe a sweater.
- An evening at the County Club would call for a more dressy look such as flannel slacks, a sporty jacket with a shirt and tie.
- For an art show or casual outing, a good look would be jeans and sport shirt or even a light jacket or sweater and some comfortable walking shoes. The idea is called relaxing but relaxing in style.
- Jogging and running have become so popular that they have developed fashions of their very own. Joggers no longer wear the old gray sweatshirt but now you see many well styled sweats worn with matching jackets.
- Racquetball players dress as colorful as tennis players.
- There is nothing wrong with a man wanting to look as young or as attractive as he can.
- Choosing a golf or sport outfit is where you can really get some of the beautiful colors for men.
- Sweaters are a great look and add beautiful colors as well as patterns in a great many varieties. Look for one that is not only warm but fashionable as well.
- No man has to look dull, dowdy and dingy now days while playing tennis, racquetball or golf for there is a large variety of beautiful colors and plaids to choose from. When choosing plaid be sure that you check the side seams, front inset, and the inset in the back for a perfect match.
- Out of season clothes should be stored in garment bags.

TIME-TESTED FASHIONS FOR MEN

- There are several fashions for men that are time tested. That is they are classic and have been around for many years without change. One example is the tuxedo jacket. It has basically the same cut today as it did 50 years ago. The width of the lapel and length of the jacket may have fluctuated but the look has remained very consistent giving the man a long lean appearance.
- Another example of a time tested outfit is the oxford shirt, a pair of khaki trousers, sweater and a navy blue blazer, as well as the popular penny loafer. If you keep this in mind, these would be good purchases and a man might get many years of use out of them without ever being fashion dated
- The smart man will buy a few high quality well made classic garments rather than buying several inexpensive and faddish items. Good clothes not only last longer but are more versatile as well.

HAIR AND GROOMING

- A well planned and good grooming routine is vital to the man who cares about his appearance. No matter whether it is short hair or the longer styles, a good hair cut and cleanliness is essential. An unkempt haircut will make you look ragged all over.
- Statistics show that the more hair that a man has on his face, the less credibility he has.
- A man's appearance should be as simple and uncomplicated as possible.
- Since after shave has alcohol in it, the scent will not linger as long as you may desire so use some body talc in the same scent to extend the aroma.
- A man needs a guide to a healthy complexion as well as the woman. If a man will take good of his skin he can have a healthy glowing complexion.
- Some of the skin experts suggest to their clients that they have a professional facial at least four times a year.
- Follow a daily cleansing and moisturizing program at home.
- To help the wrinkles that develop under and around the eyes, use a good eye cream.
- Shaving is the main difference between men and women's skins and makes men's skins tougher and more sensitive.
- Shaving removes dead surface cells.
- The skins appearance, whether men or women's relies heavily on the blood supply and the support of collagen and elastin so if these things are kept in good condition, it will increase youthful looks. Unfortunately, these resources decline and the aging process continues.
- Some factors that contribute to this process are diet, insufficient sleep, smoking, alcohol, drugs, seasonal changes, exposure to the sun, pollution, indoor heating, air-conditioning, and stress.
- If a man will shave properly, it will help the man's face rather than harm it.

HERE ARE A FEW HINTS FOR SHAVING.

- Do not use a dull blade.
- Use cream and gel preparations that work into the face and soften the facial hairs. The softer the hairs the less irritation will result on the skin.
- When using an electric shaver, the drier your skin is the better because this will cause less irritation and fewer ingrown hairs.
- Do not shave over and over an area. Once is enough.
- Keep your electric shaver clean with a small brush.
- Try to shave only once a day. If you must shave for an occasion a second time, then use only an electric shaver.
- If you will alternate between an electric shaver and a razor, it will help to reduce skin irritation.
- If your skin gets particularly irritated, cease shaving for awhile and grow a beard to let the skin rest.

- The difference between an electric shaver and a razor is the electric shaver clips the hairs off while a razor slices. Both can harm the face if not used properly on a carefully prepared face.
- Do not use talc on your face — it clogs pores.
- Men can use a good moisturizing cream instead of shaving lotion if they need more lubrication and less drying effect.

BEARDS AND MUSTACHES

- If a man is going to grow a beard or mustache, then it is important to keep it well groomed.
- A new beard should be kept clean at all times and soap and water is probably enough at the initial stages but later the beard should be washed with shampoo.
- A beard is not a form of protection for your face so cleanliness is imperative so that you do not harbor bacteria at the root of your beard.
- If flaking occurs do not use dandruff shampoo. It is probably caused by insufficient rinsing of the beard after shampooing or not drying the beard correctly.
- Blow dryers are too intense a heat for drying because of the tender facial skin.
- When you comb or brush a beard do so in the direction you want it to lie. This is almost always a downward motion.
- Trimming beards and moustaches is easier when they are dry since you can see more clearly what you are clipping away.
- To trim a full beard brush up and comb out and remove the tangles in the beard with your fingers. A rough comb or brush can break the hair and irritate the face.
- It is better to be safe than sorry when trimming so go slow and do a little at a time for if you make a mistake, the only way to correct the error is to reduce all other areas to the same length. Also, sometimes when the beard is trimmed too short the whiskers may curve in becoming itchy and possibly ingrown.
- If you want a shaped beard, be sure the line between the shaved and non shaved areas is straight, sharp and clean.
- Do not rub after shave lotion or cologne into a beard or mustache. These products are usually alcohol based and will cause the whiskers to dry out robbing them of their natural oils.
- If you are tired of a beard or mustache and want to remove it, first remove most of the hair with scissors before shaving because the razor pull can be to much leaving some severe abrasions on your face.

HAIR

- Baldness is something men dread as much as women dread a wrinkle. Thyroid and anemia can be a couple of causes and should be checked out by a doctor. However, much of baldness is found in the same family from generation to generation.
- Because hair grows according to an established cycle, some daily loss of hair is a healthy sign indicating that the ongoing process of hair replenishment is taking place.

- Doctors say that there is no actual proof that changes in diet or mineral and vitamin supplements can alter the course of hair loss as well as external shampoos directly applied to the scalp. There is some controversy over this because some companies make other claims. Redken has some products out and the theory is that calcium builds up on the scalp keeping the hair follicle from growing and the product helps to cleanse and eliminate this problem. The theory is that if the pore of the hair itself is cleansed thoroughly and not plugged up then the hair will grow.
- Many men claim that they actually do find their hair growing more healthy again when using some of the remedies and doctors say the explanation may be that some of the stress is gone over the hair loss.
- If it is a real problem in your life, there are some really wonderful toupees that you can not tell the difference when worn.
- Sometimes men wear the large mutton chop sideburns to compensate for the loss of hair on top, but it doesn't. It tends to throw off the entire balance of the face and can even emphasize more what is missing.
- Sometimes men will grow their hair to almost shoulder length to camouflage but this does not help baldness either.
- What looks the most natural is what is best.
- If you hair is getting thin on the top you can let it grow a little longer than normal but to take long hair and try to comb it over the baldness only emphasizes the problem.
- The best way to beat baldness is to accept it and accept yourself and emphasize all your other assets. Maybe baldness is an asset to you. It didn't hurt Yul Brenner or Sean Connery.
- It is important for a man to smell as good as the woman and there are many very pleasant scents out now especially for the man. Something appealing but not overpowering.
- Fragrances, hair and skin preparations and bronzes help to give a man that confident feeling. There is nothing wrong with a man wanting to look as attractive or as young as he can.

The way we dress does make a difference not only in how people look at us but how we feel about ourselves. When you go to a gathering of some sort and see a man wearing trousers that are wrinkled and too short with bright socks, you do not automatically say that must be a nice guy I want to meet him. Whether it is fair or not a person's first judgment of others is what they see displayed on the outside.

If you are skeptical about how clothes can affect your image think about how the television industry not only uses clothing but hair style and color to produce the kind of character for their movie or advertisement. It has been shown that long hair is very sensuous, blonds have more fun and that gray hair on a woman no matter how lovely she may be makes her look older.

However, gray hair on men makes them look distinguished. Glasses add an error authority and make one look like a book worm or at least like they are very intelligent.

There is no getting around the fact that we are judged by our appearance and many psychotherapists agree that up to 90% of what people remember is through nonverbal communication such as body language and facial expression as well as hair, posture, and clothes.

This does not mean that we all have to be clones of one another but where we live and what kind of work we have chosen should affect how we dress. It is important to gain some knowledge and know what to wear that is right for us and what is proper to wear in the various situations we are thrust into. That is the key to looking well put together and improving our image.

CHAPTER 4

Proverbs 31:25
"She is clothed with strength and dignity."
NIV

WOMEN: MAKING THE MOST OF YOUR DOLLAR WITH CLOTHING

When we feel good about ourselves and do not have to worry about if we are put together properly, then we can forget ourselves and give to another person. That is what truly makes us beautiful.

So many women want to add something special to their rather dull and drab fashion selections but they do not know where to start so they do nothing. Hopefully this book will give you some knowledge and confidence to be able to spend your money for something you know you can pull into your present wardrobe and get the maximum use out of it.

It is fun and exciting to go up the ladder of fashion and improve ourselves in some way.

PROFESSIONAL DRESS AND COORDINATION

- One of the things that saves money and helps your closet expand in its versatility is learning how to properly coordinate your wardrobe.
- Always purchase your first basic suits in the neutral and basic colors to blend further in your wardrobe. A navy suit will go A lot further and look more professional than a purple one.

- Investment dressing can stretch your budget and consists of selecting items that will work together with interchangeable fabrics.
- If you will learn to buy basics and separates that will move from one look into another then they will provide a multitude of looks year after year by adding a new blouse, new belt and a variety of other accessories. The cost becomes considerable less than buying a completely new outfit every year.
- Unmatched suits with a mixture of textures are very fashionable and a good way to extend your wardrobe and make it more fashionable.
- Developing a professional image will vary depending on your job, position, where you live and also what the dress code may be at your company. However, never dress down to look more dowdy, and dull. Be a leader in looking professional..
- The cuffs of a blouse should show a small amount underneath a jacket.
- Although a good suit or the look with a jacket is essential for an executive, many of the other jobs in the office may allow for a more casual look. It has been said however to dress for the job you want not the job you have. quote.
- Study the fashion magazines for putting together some good suited looks. Look around your office and get some tips from those that you admire in their dress.
- You do not have to copy. Learn some good ways to put some fashion looks together as well as what not to do.
- If you need a suit look for fabrics that are not stiff or shiny.
- Choose a fabric that can be worn year round to get the most for your money. Choose something that can be moved through your wardrobe and will go with a multitude of fabrics. Some good examples are wool blends, gabardine, natural silk and some silk blends as well as some polyester blends. Do not get polyester knit.
- The gabardine look has proven to me to be the best fabric for year round wearing and moves very nicely into dresses and other combinations.
- When buying a suit the inside should look as well made as the outside. Look for quality finishing and there should be no loose threads or raw edges showing.
- Top stitching on a jacket should be the same color as the suit for maximum versatility.
- Choose a suit that is simple. Avoid the cluttered look of extra pockets, flaps, a lot of extra buttons etc.
- Look for the sleek and classic lines
- Use your own personal touches and personality to jazz up a suit.
- A lace jabot (the lace down the front of a blouse added for extra softness) used with an old fashioned cameo pin at the neck will add a very feminine touch.
- If your figure can handle belts try belting the jacket on the outside.
- Recent studies have revealed that women who wear slacks to work regularly remain in the secretarial pool longer than those who dress up in skirts and coordinated jackets.
- In the work place, it is important not to wear any sheer see through fabrics or cling form fitting styles and of course no outfits so small that you burst the seams. Save the more casual things for leisure time, vacation, and evening.

- Do not wear jangling charm bracelets or long dangling earrings to the office and many business advisors still frown on ankle chains or bracelets. Exceptions would be people in the fashion industry.
- Your clothing affects your own moods at least as much as it does that of the person looking at you.
- It is interesting to notice that when you wear a more business look your language tends to follow your image but when you are wearing casual clothes your language tends to become more casual. It has been shown that if you decide to stay home on a drizzling afternoon and perhaps write a letter and you wear a crisp clean blouse and slacks your letter will reflect a different mood than if you are all bundled up in something warm and cozy. Be aware when you change your clothing just how it affects you. For instance, when you put on an apron, does it change your mood?
- The message that we convey with our clothing should harmonize with our personality. People read your clothing message and if you look like one of the employees when you are actually the boss, then some of your credibility with people may be lost.
- When people look at us they are not looking to see if we are thicker in the waist then we should be or if we are wearing last seasons style but what they like to see when they look at a person is a harmonious image. What you say with your clothing should enhance your personality.
- If you develop a consistency of taste and image then you will find that your wardrobe begins to expand itself with many changes. In the beginning you will have to think every match through very carefully rather than having the luxury of it just happening.
- A good basic rule is to mix one expensive, quality item with something of lesser quality.
- Another good idea is to wear the most expensive item near your face.
- You can usually get away with a less expensive skirt if it fits real well because most people do not study a skirt when you are seated or moving but the superior look in a fabric or the unique tailoring in a blouse or jacket will enhance your image.
- One thing that makes a blouse look expensive is the fine detail it may have on the collars and cuffs.
- Always check the sleeve length carefully of a jacket. A jacket or coat sleeve should be just long enough to cover the top of the wrist bone letting your blouse cuff peek out a quarter of an inch.

It is interesting to note that statistics show that how high one goes on the ladder of success is definitely connected with the way he or she dresses, wears their hair and the general overall appearance.

People form a first impression of the business where he or she works by what the people look like that greet the future client. This says that the receptionist should really have it put together and she should put her best foot forward. Many people think that how they do a job is all that is important and of course it is, but the look of professionalism is high on the amount of credibility that is given to the firm. The overall look or appearance of an executive woman is important but there is more variety in the professional dress now than you would think. It is a known fact that in this highly competitive business world, appearance does count. There are very few professional situations where a woman can just wear anything and expect to succeed or go up the ladder in that corporate structure.

Women have more freedom now in how they dress and wear their hair, however this does not mean that it is not important to look well groomed and professional. Some of the current attitudes that were studied in Calif. and New York area showed that intelligence was held to be very important in female executives as well as efficiency, friendliness and assertiveness. A lot of those surveyed believed that the stiff business suit was no longer the only acceptable way to dress for business. Dresses, skirts, and blazers were mentioned as proper business clothing. Slacks were not as desirable. Any becoming hair style seemed OK. but the longer the hair hanging on a woman's shoulders, the lower was the rating.

Our clothing is judged by more people than will ever see our home, our families or even our car and so it is an important means for one human being to make an impression on another.

I can hear some of you protesting right now saying that it just isn't fair and questioning that everyone must be so shallow and snobbish that to succeed we must look a certain way.

If you have suits in your closet that you just don't seem to be getting maximum use of then try the suit jackets with different skirts and pants checking out all possible combinations. Your closet has to be cleaned out before you can do this effectively.

Begin to build around the things that you have in your wardrobe such as building around a good standby suit with different blouses and accessories. If you are not wearing something because it is dull and uninteresting this is a good way to make it feel new.

JACKETS

- Jackets are an important item of clothing to have in your wardrobe. When you have an interview they add presence to you as a person and they are an important addition to credibility in meetings or a presentation of a speech.
- A jacket gives upper body presence but there are other things that also add to your appearance and that is the pearl earring or a quality necklace.

DRESSES, SUITS

- Dresses are being worn more than in the past so a nice tailored dress in gabardine or jersey with the soft shoulder padding would be an good option.
- In the business world, choose a three piece suit in your best dark basic, your second suit in your best light neutral, and a third suit in one of your best coordinating colors. This will give you a workable interchangeable coordinated beginning.The color pink

in business is good in a blouse but in an all over suit it has shown not to be as professional. The experts say that it does not show enough authority. However the muted mauve pink and muted fuchsia lend quality to the look of a garment. The powder pink or shocking pink would not be as good. Your overall presentation including a briefcase, handbag and shoes is important, so all should be of quality.Grooming is very important and completes the polished look. That is why unpolished shoes, unkempt hair and dirty uncleaned clothing can make the most expensive clothes look unprofessional.

- You may have to spend some money to acquire a basic wardrobe but once you have it, it will cost you less to maintain than you would spend buying lost of unrelated pieces. Although there may be a special occasion or event that requires a special purchase, a basic wardrobe should be able to met at least 95% of your clothing needs.
- Don't forget to add some vests to your wardrobe. You will be surprized at how a special vest can totally make a dull drab outfit very special.
- Clothes are a part of those split second first impressions and they might mean the difference between a positive and a negative impression.
- Investment dressing can stretch your budget and consists of selecting items that will work together with interchangeable fabrics.If you do not have any suits you will probably have to invest in a couple of basic ones in color and line. They are always good because you can separate the pieces and make several other good looking fashions.
- Get one suit in a neutral color such as blue, navy, grey and then add the other one in a small muted plaid or tweed. Then you can go from office to dinner meetings with a minimum change.

Choose complimentary fabrics and styles so that you can mix jackets and skirts. If you have a dress or a couple of basic skirts in coordinating colors then it will help to expand your wardrobe. Be sure that the fabric in the suits is a year round fabric that can be worn well with other fabrics and moved through your wardrobe to dresses. Such a fabric would be gabardine and some of your nice wool blends but pure wool is harder to move through your wardrobe and does not wear well in spring and summer.Pure linen suits wrinkle very badly.To go to an after-dinner business meeting wear your basic suit skirt and add a softer cardigan knit and some nice pearls to complete a very nice look very simply.You could also complete a nice evening look with a pair of colored hosiery and a dressier pair of shoes.Be very aware of the shoes that you put with your outfits because they can ruin a balanced look. If you can afford only one or two pairs of shoes choose the versatile pump, and for evening you can add some of the shoe accessories that they have out now.The high rubber wedge shoe or dressy shoe with straps is not a professional look.

WOMEN'S JACKETS

- When you start purchasing in the fall and have a limited budget, the best purchase for your wardrobe will be a new jacket especially if you are working. It will be the most important and expensive thing you buy so make it the highest quality you can afford. If you do not work, it can be an important item in the wardrobe for meetings, church, etc.

- When purchasing the jacket be sure that it is versatile in line and that it will go over several different shirts, slacks and dresses in your wardrobe.
- Types of jackets to consider are the tailored look, the cardigan which falls straight and without buttons. It can be short or long. The easy shirt jacket and the blouson jacket are good looks to consider. This jacket usually is bloused over the dierrere and longer style which is good for many figures.
- Another good jacket rule is to buy a solid jacket to go with most of your tweed or patterned skirts and pants. Then buy another jacket with a different shape in a pattern like a subtle tweed or plaid to go with the other half of your wardrobe which includes skirts and pants that are solid. That makes it easy to stay within two color families that are compatible and you can intermix and always be able to finish the look of each outfit with a jacket.
- Next purchase should be a pretty skirt and blouse that match and put together to look like a dress but as separates they will be wearable in so many different ways. It is best to get them in a subtle interesting color that you are working with in your wardrobe and get a soft sweater and some nice slacks in a complementarily color. Then you will have four pieces to be able to mix and match with an endless variety. A tweed jacket that will go with all four items will take you even further in your wardrobe.

DRESSY CLOTHES

- Simplicity is an elegant look and the feeling of being fashionable can be achieved through the wise choice of fabric, color and design when you are choosing a party dress.
- The dressy fabrics such as silks, satins, panne velvet, lace and subtle metallic in black and gold will be very dressy.
- If you can wear black it is always a good evening elegant look.
- You can take a good pair of wool crepe slacks and wear them sporty in the day with a tweed blazer and then just change to a gold flecked blouse and metallic belt to make it more dressy for night.
- Another suggestion for an evening look would be a skirt that is soft and narrow and ankle long with a soft tunic top or beautiful blouse or even a camisole and small quilted jacket.
- Those tops could also be worn with a soft silk pajama pant for a completely different look.
- Evening wear separates are more versatile than a dress or gown that has only one look. When money is an issue something that is versatile is a key word.
- Whenever you are in a store keep your eyes open for clothing pieces that have the potential to be made more formal.
- If you wear a fur for evening and it gets wet, shake gently to remove excess moisture then hang on a sturdy wooden hanger in a well ventilated area away from the heat.

ACCESSORIES

- Remember that a more bold accessory at the waist means less accessorizing at the neck.
- Pretty sweaters look even more beautiful sometimes when an antique collar is added.
- To dress down a suit add some sporty earrings.
- To dress up a suit button it up, leave the blouse off, and wear some jewelry that is a little more sparkle. This could go into evening also.
- The right accessories are important. However, no wardrobe looks good if there is a lax in good personal grooming habits.
- If you have a very mundane sweater or blouse try changing to a different type of button that may give it an entirely different look. You could make it sporty this way or more dressy.
- If you have a dress or skirt that is to long cut off the hem and make into a long wide cummerbund sash for the waist which will give you a whole new look.
- If your skirt is a bit on the short side and you feel uncomfortable in it being so short, then try wearing stockings of the same color as the skirt and this will make the skirt look longer.
- You can update your blouses, dresses and suits by adding shoulder pads.
- A blouse and a skirt that is of a different color can be turned into an interesting outfit by adding a scarf or a shawl that has the same two colors in its print.
- Don't clutter an elegant look with too bright an accent of scarf or jewelry.
- The color of an accessory can either coordinate with an outfit or it can add a neat look of contrast. For instance a blue knit dress, soft blue tinted hose, and blue shoes might be boring so to be more exciting try wearing a bright contrasting color at the waist or neck
- Vary your blouses with suits with V necklines and soft bows at the neck.
- If you want to wear the latest fashion touch such as a vest, then do not also wear the latest hat, latest stockings, latest stick pin etc.
- Stand in front of a full length mirror and notice what is catching your eye the most and this can give you lots of ideas on correct accessorizing.
- When you are adding an accent to an outfit such as a collar, cuffs, yolks and insets, experiment with mixes of florals, plaids and stripes
- Consider wearing a beautiful silk shirt over another silk blouse using it as kind of a jacket.
- Poor accessories can make a very classy outfit look very cheap. Accessories refer to everything except the main garment.
- Nail polish is an accessory and should be considered in your total look because your hands are displayed and seen by all. If you do not wear polish, your nails should be well groomed, buffed, clean and filed.
- When choosing accessories, choose ones that harmonize with each other and that can be worn with more than one outfit.
- Purchase all accessories with your personality in mind.

- Don't try to copy someone if it is not you.
- Be a collector of good accessories and choose them for how long they will last.
- It is fun to keep up with the changing fads, but invest the most money in the classics such as good jewelry and good leather.
- Too many accessories or points of interest will cheapen the whole look so strive for simplicity. However, most people under accessorize.
- Accessories play an important role in the plan of dressing fashionable and can help you get a maximum mileage from a small compact wardrobe as well as provide new life for old classics.
- Pearls are a real basic and classic item for a wardrobe and are always a good purchase.
- Adding lace collars and cuffs to a blouse or sweater you already own is a very pretty update.
- A good way to update something old is with the addition of color. Fashion magazines will clue you into the latest color hues of the season.
- You can have the look of something new by adding the latest colors to your wardrobe in small doses such as a red scarf or orange belt.
- Update your clothes by wearing them differently than you have in the past. For instance shove the sleeves up the arm for a new look from the neatly folded and cuffed look.
- T-shirts are a classic but to change the look knot them in the front or wear as one layer under a blouse or dress.
- If pants are shorter for this season, then simply take up the hem a few inches and you have the new season look.
- Work on some new tricks by experimenting with various looks and come up with your own signature style.
- If you buy an outfit that has a seasonless fabric then you can wear it with western boots or with sandals in the spring.
- Slight switches in jewelry and scarves make many outfits look very different.
- To achieve a new look with your old blouses try rolling up the sleeves to just below the elbow and turn up your collar.
- Take a vest that usually goes with a three piece suit you bought and wear it with other things.
- Accessories are like the icing on a cake because they add sparkle and interest to clothes that would otherwise be just a dress or just a blouse. They change a look from day to evening or from winter to summer. They are an inexpensive way for you to update your clothing into the new looks of the season without major purchases.
- A good rule to use when buying accessories is to add color where it will create a very dramatic effect. Adding color in two or three places is still o.k. but when you get more than that, the look becomes very busy for the eye to appreciate unless it is tastefully combined with color value and intensity.
- One rule you will hear from the experts is to put on all the accessories that you want to wear and then take one off. It is better to have too few than too many.

- Some good accessories to consider adding to your wardrobe are belts, scarves, blouses, shawls, vests, hats, jewelry, handkerchiefs, flowers, hosiery and shoes.
- A good rule of thumb is that any color in an accessory should be balanced by one more touch of that same color in another accessory. When you get too many color touches it can take away the balance such as a red handbag, red shoes and red belt.
- It is important to keep your accessories in proportion and size to the silhouette of your outfit.
- Use accessories to play up your good points and play down your bad points. For instance, if your waistline is not your best asset, the do not use waist accessories.
- To give a sweater a different look, wear a pullover sweater on the outside and belt it for a change.
- When adding a men's tie accessory to a blouse, to keep it from looking too masculine, do not tie it too close to the neck but let the tie drop down a bit in a softer knot.
- Another hint, in wearing the tie look, choose a paisley print and add a strand or two of pearls draped over the top.
- A sweater dress is a fun item of clothing to accessorize. Instead of the same old look with delicate chains and self belts, try add a more dramatic look with a beautiful burnished copper belt.
- Try a new look with a sweater jacket, either the blazer type or cable knit type.
- Try adding a tweed one and update with slight shoulder padding.
- Add one of the large multicolored scarves or shawls and drape over your shoulder or even use as a hip wrap.
- Don't forget the beautiful and bold looking gold and silver jewelry they have and add to your wardrobe in necklaces, earrings and bracelets.
- Try adding some really classy belts to some of your slacks If your waist can take it, make it wide and in an interesting material like snake skin or suede.
- Try a cummerbund with a braided overbelt in a contrasting color.
- Silk dresses are fun to accessorize. Perk one up with a pretty sweater vest. Be sure that you have some of the color of the dress in the vest.
- A blazer is also a nice addition and will change the look entirely.
- Another accessory that has become very popular is the artificial nail.
- Elegant longer nails add length to your fingers if they do not get so long that they become a topic of conversation and ridicule.

ACCESSORIZING FOR YOUR PERSONALITY

- Mood accessorizing is an example of how our personality will help us to accessorize to fit how we feel about ourselves. Not everyone is going to feel good in the same accessories and many times we look foolish when we try to imitate something that is not our personality.
- Sporty people look and feel good in leather, boots, shoulder bags, wool scarves.
- For the very feminine people, the key word is delicate such as dainty chains, delicate stones, high strappy heels, tinted hosiery, silk flowers and soft flowing scarves.

- The glamorous look calls for glitter, metallics, copper, rhinestones, high heeled sandals, beaded bags, and dangling earrings.
- Dramatic people like to get their point across with color such as bright red , fuchsia, yellow, purples, turquoise. They look and feel good in large accent makers such as a shawl, a wide hip sash and some of the larger more dramatic looking jewelry.
- The business woman in a more conservative and classic look will like gold jewelry, neat shoulder or clutch bags with the matching pump and beautiful leather belts. The suit is a comfortable piece of clothing for her.
- If you have had a wide silver bracelet in your drawer for sometime but whenever you wear it you feel uncomfortable, you may be a different personality type than the bracelet conveys. Study yourself and discover your own style that will make you comfortable when wearing it.

SCARVES AND SHAWLS

- Large geometric scarves and shawls add interest to a wardrobe. Remember proportion when you are buying. Taller women can wear the much larger scarf and print.
- Add to your wardrobe to keep up to date such as important accessories of the season. Pearls and scarves are always good purchases.
- When adding an accessory such as a scarf to the wardrobe, use it to blend into a last years closet of clothes. It can also be used as an accent near the face when something that you have purchased is not the best color for you. Scarves can be a great addition to your wardrobe if they are well chosen. Silk is the best fabric for tying.
- A silk square look very good tied and neatly tucked into a sweater.
- If you have a high neckline, a scarf can work well tied around the outside of a collar and knotted.
- Long cashmere scarves are a real good accessory with coats and jackets.
- Shawls can look quite smart when they are draped over suits, dresses and even coats.
- Remember to keep proportion in mind when choosing scarves and shawls.
- Shawls can be a real asset to the larger figured woman and large hips because this can be an attractive camouflage.
- Wearing scarves and shawls takes practice. Play with them in front of a full length mirror so that you can see where they are the greatest asset to you.
- Be aware of the fabric when you purchase a scarf or a shawl because some knot easier and are less bulky.
- Test the draping ability, whether they look stiff or hand limp.
- Check for proportion when you look in the mirror and see if the scarf makes you look top heavy and is the effect uplifting.
- The only way that a scarf or shawl looks good is if it looks effortless and natural. Otherwise do not wear it.
- Do not tug or pull at the scarf accessory but put it in place and then pin it so that you can forget about it.
- When you purchase, remember the colors you are working with in your wardrobe because this is where you can add an accent of color to an otherwise drab outfit.

- Collect both solids and prints and the small men's wear tie designs on silk scarves always look great for business.
- Look for little checks or flowers on silk or cotton scarves for summertime.
- The larger flowers and prints are best on the larger scarves.
- Usually the rule to follow is the smaller the scarf the smaller the print or pattern.
- Be sure to look for hand rolled or machine rolled edges on the scarves.
- If the edges are fringed, they should be at least l/2 inches deep on silk scarves, shawls and even more of an edge on wool. The finish on a scarf or shawl is very important.
- Fabrics such as silk, crepe de chine, and cashmere are always good buys and make an outfit look more expensive.
- When you neck and waist tie, fold in thirds because the scarf will become less bulky, holds, and wraps the body better since you are using the bias of the fabric to do the tying.
- It is important for you not to be afraid to use these items to accessorize because they add pizazz for not too much money.
- The more neck length that you want to create the lower you tie the scarf.
- The shorter you are the smaller the scarf.
- Do not hesitate to mix gold and silver jewelry with pearls to give an entirely new look.
- Scarves in polka dots, animal prints and sea motifs can update an outfit for that season if those designs are prevalent.
- Some of the smaller scarves can be used as a pocket accent by letting them drape over the top like a pretty handkerchief.
- A very tailored shirt can be brightened and made more feminine with a soft grosgrain ribbon tied into a bow at the top of the collar or use an attractive coordinated scarf tied in a bow.
- Add a bright touch with a handkerchief sticking out of a pocket. Be sure that your bustline can take this look. Scarves can work magic by tying a scarf at the waist or even a twist of a bright scarf at your neck for a burst of color.
- If you have a large square scarf, you can sling it over your shoulder as a shawl.
- Detachable lace collars can change the whole look of a blouse or dress and add some femininity.
- Don't forget the feminine touch of a lace handkerchief peaking out of your jacket or shirt pocket.
- Make good use of a pretty shawl or lacy scarf and drape it around your shoulder.
- Tie a soft feminine chiffon scarf in a soft bow at your neck.
- Scarves are a very important part of your wardrobe and are a means of bringing the right color to your face.
- One of the secrets to wearing a scarf is having it secure to your garment so use pins that do not show underneath to keep a scarf in place or you could also fasten it with a beautiful brooch.

- Even if you have a short neck you can wear a scarf — just do not tie it directly around the neck and keep the fabric soft and not too bulky. Tie scarves that drape downward and not too close to the neckline.
- A basic dress can go from morning to evening simply by adding a clever scarf accessory.
- Try using a long multicolored scarf sashed around your waist to add color during the day and then switch to a softer printed silk scarf for evening and add some dressy jewelry.
- A big oversized scarf is a really good investment and can be used so many ways. You can sling it over your shoulder and belt it in place at your waist. This looks good with slacks as well as skirts and dresses.
- You can fold a shawl in half diagonally and wrap around the neck in lose folds like a cowl neckline.
- It can also be tied sarong style on the top to make a n instant exotic blouse. Then add a bright jacket and you have a brand new look.
- Scarves are a great way to accent a pretty neck as well as enhance the face. You can bring your best colors up to your face and create some softness.
- Everyone can wear scarves regardless of age or size if they are worn in the correct manner. Just keep your proportions in mind and where you want the accent.
- A person with a short neck would not wear scarves right under her chin but a longer slightly dropped scarf would be excellent.
- A person with a longer neck can wear the scarves directly on the neck and horizontal ties across the neckline will shorten and add width.
- Always carefully remove the label from a scarf before wearing it.

BELTS

- Belts are good purchases if your waist can take the look because they add a very classic simple and fashionable touch to your wardrobe. A rule of thumb on a belt is that it must be of excellent quality. You are much better off with fewer belts all of quality such as leather than many cheap ones.
- You can make a moderately priced dress that comes with a self tie belt which tends to downgrade the look immediately by adding a neat looking belt. This can change a dress from chintzy to classy.
- Generally speaking belts should be in varying shades of the neutrals and basics you are coordinating with. Tans and natural leather for instance blend very nicely while belts in contrasting colors can be effective they will also emphasize the waistline.
- If you an ardent belt wearer, wonderful interchangeable belt buckles are worth considering.
- If you want to blouse a top or dress over a belt, before belting, lift your shoulders as high as possible and while your shoulders are lifted, belt. You then have an even excess of fabric about the belt so then when you relax your shoulders you will have the perfect bloused amount.
- Think of a suit like a dress and add fashion touches like belts and lapel pens.

- Some good basic accessories to have in your wardrobe are:
- Good leather belts. Even a suit or skirt looks more finished with a nice belt.
- A good buy would be a l/2 to 3/4 inch wide belt in a neutral color to wear with skirts and pants when the blouse is tucked in.
- For a dressier look you might like to add a gold
- or silver belt in the metal of your season to give the waistline a finished and dressier look.
- Use your imagination to create unusual and striking belts like try winding scarves around your waist.
- Add some unique belt buckles to your belts as well as adding flowers and brooches.
- If your waist cannot take a belted look, then use a skinny belt in metal with a smaller belt buckle, which could peep out from under a vest or a jacket.
- A soft leather free form belt is a fun accessory that you can tie into many different positions.

NYLONS

- You might want to change the look of your entire outfit by adding a new pair of textured hosiery.
- When wearing boots, try to wear the hose color the same as your boot to prevent too many breaks in the line.
- Nylon is strengthened from cold so rinse your hose in ice water, dry them, and then store them in your freezer and they will last much longer.
- One interesting accessory to consider and maybe you never thought of it as an accessory is hosiery. Do not wear white or the lighter hosiery if you legs are heavy even if the fashion of the season is showing it. Wear an unassuming hosiery that does not draw attention to the leg. Taupe for cool skinned people and suntan for warm tones are always good.
- Blend your nylon into your shoe for the best elongated and non choppy look and it is a better fashion look also. Therefore wear black with black shoes and it will give you a longer look. If in doubt on a hosiery color wear taupe for cool colors and suntan for warm colors. The fashion industry breaks this rule however with some fad fashion looks by putting white nylons with a black or navy shoe but unless you have a nicely shaped leg this is not the best look for you. Remember the eye goes to the lightest or brightest thing on your body first.19. Women with nice shapely legs can wear the pinstripes, tweeds, and herringbone hosiery.
- Darker shades of hosiery will diminish the heavier leg.
- When you wear a neutral tone hosiery, it will make your legs look slightly tanned.
- The wool-like textured stocking that is the same color as your outfit gives a nice sporty look. Navy opaque hose with a black skirt and sweater is a good example. It is not too good to pick up a minor color in your outfit with your hosiery.
- Do not wear the reinforced toe nylons with open toed shoes.
- The size of your hand bag should be in proportion to your size.

- To help your panty hose last longer, try adding a few drops of liquid fabric softener to the final rinse water.

SHOES

- Shoes are an accessory that makes a big difference not only in adding to your fashion look but the correct shoe can add to the attractiveness of the leg.
- Shoes bought in your prevalent basic or neutral rather than a color will go further in your wardrobe.
- Don't forget that shoes are one of your most important accessories.
- Take your shoes to the shoe shop and have them put nylon caps on the heels to protect them.
- Don't forget that some of your most important accessories are your shoes.
- Unless you want someone to look at your feet first, then do not wear a shoe lighter than the hem of your garment such as white with a navy skirt. A brighter shoe such as red is a nice accent however.
- Shoes with slingback heels that show more foot are good and give a younger look than the closed pumps. A lighter weight higher pump is a younger look than the heavy low pump.
- A shoe can add to or detract from a nice outfit. In choosing a shoe, remember proportion in heel height. Generally speaking a good rule is the longer the skirt the higher the heel. However, you will see the fashion industry break this rule and when it is a fashion trend it looks o.k.
- Moccasins, modified slippers, flat boots and sandals are classic in the shoe line and have been around for ever.
- Most women look better with a little heel rather than too flat a shoe. The women that wear the flat shoe best are the taller women that are evenly proportioned.
- Don't wear a flat shoe just because it is in fashion but choose what is best for your leg and height.
- The best investment is a low cut classic pump made of the finest calfskin. You will get a lot of mileage out of this shoe.
- Fine leather pumps are perfect for any season and are adaptable to any time of the day.
- Suede or patent are very beautiful but they are not as versatile and would be a better buy as a second or third pair of shoes.
- The Chanel two toned slingback shoe is a wonderful classic and always look smart. This would be a great choice for a second pair of shoes.
- To get the most for your money always consider color in your purchase and it should be the color of the basic or neutral that you are working with in your wardrobe. Brightly colored handbags and shoes are fun but they are impractical unless you have a large clothing budget.
- An exception for a basic or neutral shoe would be among the casual shoes like a purple or red sandal.

- White shoes tend to make the foot look larger so bone or taupe would be a better choice for your wardrobe. White looks best with white outfits.
- Shoes should never make the statement of your outfit but should add to the elegance of an outfit.
- This is a natural healing tip. Hasten and soothe the healing of blisters on your feet by rubbing them with clean, fresh cut grass. Another natural healing tip is to purchase an aloe vera plant and break a leaf and use the healing substance inside to rub on blisters or burns.
- Shoes should be clean, well polished and the heels well taken care of. Have your shoe repair man put nylon caps on the heels.
- Use plastic heel protectors. It is very easy to step into a grate and gouge a hole into the heel.
- Shoes will last longer and look better if they are stored in shoe trees when not being worn.
- Anticipate which shoe you will be wearing with your outfit and polish them the night before. It might be a good idea to polish shoes all at once and then they will always be ready for you to step out in.
- Be aware of the heels of your shoes and keep them repaired so that they are not run down.
- You can purchase a heel protector to rest your heel in when you are driving or wear an old pair to drive in and put your good shoes on when you get to your destination. This will prevent those rubbing marks that you get on the back of the heel.
- Add the interesting little shoe accessories that they have now and change the look of the whole shoe.
- A clutch handbag in the reptile or snake look creates a business like look.
- To make a more masculine shoe look more feminine, wear crocheted or laced topped socks with them.
- Do not wear a strappy sandal with a tweed suit or a broad heeled pump with a dressy dress.
- If you add the wrong shoe to your outfit as well as the wrong handbag, jewelry and belt all in different styles, it makes for a very confusing fashion picture.
- For business wear, the classic pump is probably the best choice.
- Wear a shoe color that does not cause the person looking at you to see the feet first by matching the hem of the garment or darker. A lighter shoe would draw attention to the feet such as white but a brighter shoe may be a fashion accent such as red.
- In buying shoes you can minimize the ankles and slenderize the calves if you avoid ankle straps and pick a more pointed toe.
- Do not wear shiny material in shoes unless it is coordinated to an evening outfit.
- Your feet will appear slimmer if your shoes are all one color and low cut.
- If you want your ankles to look larger, then wear ankle straps, rounded or square toes, two toned shoes, buckles and bows and you will add width.
- If you will toss a sheet of fabric softener into you shoes when you store them, it will cut the odor.

- It is important that the shoe you purchase looks good on your feet, compliments your leg, be comfortable, and works well proportionately with your body and outfit. Well designed shoes are often high priced but worth the money for the overall affect they produce.
- A low cut pump or low cut slingback with a medium height and narrow heel are very flattering designs for most women and are best bets for an every day shoe. A low cut shallow shoe interferes very little with the line of the leg and gives it a long slim look.
- Shoes that have ankle straps, T-straps and straps across the instep are generally unflattering. They will interrupt the line of the leg and make it appear shorter.
- In general, the less shoe there is the better the leg will look.
- For a dressy evening occasion, a simple elegant slingback type strappy sandal will most always look good.
- Some higher heeled shoes look wonderful in the store but are impossible to walk in. Do not be tempted by the look alone because if your walk or posture is affected by a hard to walk in shoe, it will affect your whole look.
- To prevent slipping and sliding in a new pair of shoes, rub the soles with a piece of fine sandpaper to provide some traction.

BOOTS

- Boots are a fun but can be expensive accessory. They look very smart with longer skirts and with fall and winter coats.
- Do not wear them indoors however, unless they are part of the overall look you are wearing.
- When you wear skirts or dresses, boots add an extra dimension to your legs but be very careful that they do not cause extra horizontal cutting lines by showing leg between boot and hem of garment or if they are a shorter cut keep the hosiery the same color as the boot.
- Sporty type boots do not look good with the stylish dressy ensembles.
- Boots are very expensive so do not buy a trendy boot that will soon be out of style like perhaps a flat wedge. A classic style with a one or two inch heel would be the best buy.
- The silhouette should be slim and flattering to the leg.
- Also, like buying a good handbag, it should be the finest leather. Boots are one place you cannot skimp and have them keep their shape and looking attractive.
- Try to avoid a space between the top of your boot and your hemline because it will tend to shorten the leg.
- Usually boots do not look good with silk dresses because give to heavy a look.
- Boots are usually worn only in the fall and winter. The exception of course is the western boot which is worn with westernwear year round.
- Patent leather is not as good a material to buy in a boot as real leather.
- Color of the boot should be in your best dark basic that you are coordinating with that will blend into your wardrobe and with your coat. You can see how important it is for

you to be coordinated throughout your wardrobe to get the most mileage from your clothes and shoes.

- Natural leather looks good also.
- Boots should always be longer than the longest toe and that is not always the big toe.

JEWELRY

- If you have some pearls and wish to restore the shine then gently rub them with a little olive oil and wipe with a soft cloth.
- Be sure you do not get anything that has alcohol in it on your pearls such as perfume.
- Do not throw out any jewelry because generally it will come back in style and you will be able to use it again. A good example is when the rhinestones of the past came back in as strong statement in l986.
- Do not ever attempt to pierce your ears yourself or have a friend pierce them for you because the chances are the instrument she uses will not be sterile and you risk infection.
- Ear piercing is not recommended for skin that forms keloid or hard raised scar tissue.
- The gold jewelry looks best against a warm skinned person while silver, white and rose gold is best for the cool seasoned person.
- A watch may not seem like a fashion accessory but it is because it is something that you wear every day. It is an accessory that will get noticed a lot so make sure it is a sleek high quality item.
- A sporty watch does not look good with a high fashion dress and does not go into the business scene as well. If you can only purchase one watch try a medium sized semi dressy watch and a band with gold and silver in it makes. This will make the watch very versatile.
- Ropes of pearls can be used in multiples or mixed with other jewelry pieces.
- When selecting jewelry, scale it down to the size of the individual. Dainty jewelry worn on the larger woman tends to get lost on the person and too large a piece of jewelry may overpower the smaller individual.
- The cool season people look better in silver, white gold and rose gold and the warm season people look best in the yellow gold, if you have pieces that are out of your best color key just add a few pieces of the opposite metal and wear them together. Try mixing your gold and silver chains and bracelets.
- A simple loop earring is a very basic look and for those with small boned facial features, the smaller the circumference of the earring the thicker it can be. The larger the circumference , the thinner it should be.
- Rings are fun and should be scaled to the size of the hand, worn appropriately for the occasion and it is important to have your nails well manicured since rings draw attention to the hand.
- If your jewelry moves a lot or makes a lot of noise, it is usually worn in the day time or with sportswear.
- Jewelry for dressier occasions should sparkle or be of the rich gold and silver pieces.

- If you are a public speaker or leading a meeting session, be sure that you jewelry does not move and is noiseless.
- Wear only two pieces of matched jewelry at one time but the unmatched jewelry that is combined cleverly can create a very chic look.
- The brushed metal is very dressy especially if it is used with stones and pearls.
- The shiny metal is used a lot for a sporty and casual look although there are a lot of shiny metal pieces that are elegant for evening.
- If the shiny and brushed metals are combined, it makes for a less dressy look.
- If you do not like to wear a lot of jewelry, the string of pearls is a wonderful addition to a wardrobe and adds a touch of femininity
- Real pearls are desirable but sometimes that is out of our budget. A good string costume pearls will do and they are an accessory that will go anyplace and never go out of style.
- The color of pearls that go best with the various color keys are rose, soft white and gray for winter and summers and springs and autumns wear a yellow hue or cream color the very best.
- Plastic, wood, ceramic, shell, and leather jewelry is very casual and should be worn with the natural cottons and the more casual fabric and look.
- Don't forget to use lapel pens at the neckline of a blouse or dress or on a lapel to add a fresh fashion touch.
- If you like to wear bracelets do not wear them when you speak or are conducting a meeting if they jingle for they can be very distracting.
- Bracelets area really nice fashion touch and add a touch of pizazz to an outfit.
- Don't forget the touch of accessory in the hair. This is a good look when in a fashion mood but not as good in the business world.
- One good thing to remember is to not use too much gaudy jewelry. However no outfit should be totally devoid of accessories. Gaudy jewelry looks best on younger women and usually is worn with more casual or sporty clothes.
- Have a jeweler convert an unused ring or pin into a choker into a necklace This is a good tip for using a precious piece of jewelry that is seldom worn.
- Be creative with jewelry working with beads in all shapes, sizes, colors, and lengths. You will find that jewelry can spark up a dull and drab outfit like almost nothing else can.

GLOVES

- Gloves are usually purchased to keep the hands warm and clean but they are no longer used for just that purpose. They can be worn to add another dimension of fashion to your outfit.
- A good basic glove is of cloth or leather and should be neutral in color.
- Whenever a person wears white gloves the hands are the focal point of the outfit. To me it reminds me of Al Jolson and how prominent his hands were.
- The best length for a glove is a short glove and it should cover the wrist bone.

GLASSES

If you are about to start wearing glasses, there is nothing to be concerned about because today there are shapes and colors for every face shape and coloring and styles for all activities. Your lifestyle should be considered in choosing a glass frame, so whether you are a high fashion type person, preppy, or classic, there are flattering eye glasses for everyone and the way you want to look.

Many people do not like to wear glasses but they do have an effect on people. A business like frame can make a young woman look more mature and authoritative.

- Always select a frame in the correct color key for your skin tone.
- If you wear a tinted lens in your glasses be sure it is in a tone that will blend with your skin tone and makeup.
- Tinted lenses give a negative reaction when they are so dark that the person with which you are speaking cannot make eye contact.
- Another interesting accessory is a perfect pair of sunglasses. When buying sunglasses, look for strength, ultraviolet protection, comfort and freedom from distortion.
- Do not choose a frame that is the same shape as your face.
- Be careful of the color so that you pick in your color key. The color needs to go with your coordination and your skin tone. For instance you do not want a brown frame if you are coordinating in navy and gray.
- The silver frame will look best on a cool skinned person and a gold frame good with the warm skinned people.
- The shape of your face and the coloring of your skin should be considered when choosing frames.
- If you have a round face, you will want to avoid round frames which will continue to accentuate the roundness. Instead a softened square frame or oval shape would be more flattering.
- If you have a square face, then choose a rounded or oval frame. Avoid repeating the square jaw with square frames.
- It is a good idea to take someone with you when choosing a frame because they can tell you what really looks good on you. Sometimes it is hard to see glasses on your self if you are very nearsighted.
- Invest some money and get a couple different frames which you change from day to day so you do not get tired of the same look. Some different colors might be good for day or into the evening.
- Colors should be selected for skin tone and eye color and of course to go with what you are coordinating with in your wardrobe.
- Silver frames look wonderful on the cool winter people and on grey or white haired women.
- Soft blues, greens, browns and rose colors offer a lot of color choices for most women.

- Rose tones add a warmth to a sallow skin but the color should always be subtle in a soft blend.
- As we get older, the lines of the face tend to lose that upward look so it is important to choose glasses that help to lift the face. A pair of glasses with the temples turning upward can lift the whole face and are especially flattering to the profile.
- Women with larger shaped noses should look for eyeglasses where all the interest or fashion accents are at the side of the temples taking the attention away from the center of the face and the nose.
- If your eyes are close set choose an oval shape that widens or flattens out towards the sides and a color that is pale at the bridge of the nose and deepens towards the sides and outer edges.
- A long face and an angular shaped face can be shortened with a square or rounded shape and choosing glasses that are gentle in shape and color.
- When choosing glasses, think about having a total balanced look in color and frame. The right color brings a warm, healthy, natural glow to the face whereas the wrong color may make the complexion appear pale, sallow, flushed or muddy.
- If your complexion is pale try to prevent an overpowering of a delicate look. Try using powdered and icy pastels for cool skins and the light earth tone colors if you have a warm skin tone.
- The rosy complexion needs to be softened so try the blue cast cool colors and the neutrals. Avoid the reds and the pink tones.
- The olive complexion looks best in the rosy or blue cast colors in a deep, vivid or icy shade or try the clear, bright neutrals. Avoid orange, gold, and yellow green undertone colors and too much ashy tone.
- If you prefer the metal frame, the silver is best for the cool skinned person and gold for the warm skin.
- The bottom line in selecting a proper frame that you will be happy with should reflect your life style, primary wardrobe colors, and personal preference.
- Before you get a frame, determine your face shape by pulling your hair away from the face and study the outline from temple to jawline. Ask yourself if you see curves or straight lines. Curves suggest a round or heart shaped face and the straight lines suggest an oblong or square face. Also check the proportion, width and length and then choose frames that contrast with facial shape. Do not repeat the face shape with the frame. You could also take a tube of lipstick or a bar of soap and draw an outline of your face shape on the mirror and then step away and you can see where you are wide narrow and get a pretty good idea of your face shape.
- The darker the frame the smaller the face will appear.
- Light frames make the face appear as it really is.
- A frame with a high placed light color on the temple is good to lengthen a short face and a low placed, darker frame on the temple will shorten a long face.
- If your hairstyle is full and worn close to the face, try a thinner lighter frame.
- Less hair worn on the face would call for a slightly bolder frame.

- The eye wear you choose should be properly proportioned for the size and shape of your face. Too big and you look out of proportion and too small, it will make you look closed in both in eyes and face shape.
- If you have had your color key done and know your skin tone, then use your best basic and neutrals to guide you in frame tint. Cool tints are the clear soft blues and greys, taupe and silver. The warm tints are peaches, golds, and warm browns.
- The best pick me uppers for making yourself look less tired during the day and more glowing in your complexion is the application of blush with a brush and soften in.
- If you wear tinted lenses, make certain that you choose the tone as carefully as you choose the color of your makeup. If your skin is sallow or olive, steer clear of greens and yellows. If you have a ruddy complexion, avoid too much rose tone.
- If you wear contacts, use fragrance free eye make up especially mascara. Also, look for makeup without metallic flakes that may get into the eyes.
- Sunglasses are important in high glare conditions such as skiing where the light is very intense or bright driving conditions where the brightness may blind you to oncoming traffic.
- Never wear sunglasses when driving at night, in fog, rain or any other condition that already restricts visibility.
- The wisest tint choices for sunglasses are brown and sage green which probably gives the best all round protection. Other tints are neutral and smokey grey. All of these reduce the intensity but do not affect the values of the colors. Avoid the rosier tinted reds, pinks, yellows, and oranges.
- Choosing the right color glass frame is a purchase that is quite expensive and should coordinate with your wardrobe as well as blend with your skin tones.
- Take in consideration the shape of your face.
- Make a long face appear wider by choosing wider frames that cover a good portion of your face making it appear attractively shorter.
- The heart shaped face looks good in the shorter rectangular frame.
- The square face should look for frames that have soft curving lines.
- Get the best perspective of how the glasses will look by standing in front of a large preferably full length mirror. In this way you will be able to sense the proper proportions.
- Never repeat the shape in the eyeglasses that is the same as your face shape.
- Round faces look very nice when they wear frames that are deep and angular or geometrically shaped.
- An oval face look good in just about any shape frame. However, even though they can wear about any shaped frame keep in mind the individual personality.
- For sallow people, add a little cheek color at the lower outer edge of your lenses.
- A good shade for winter people is the gray blue tint but another good tint is the mauve.
- Summer people wear the glass tint of mauve, blue or gray with rose at the bottom.
- Springs look best in the soft brown tint or peachy pink.
- Autumns wear the soft brown or peachy pink.

- If you get the tints too dark, the eyes will look tired.
- When wearing a tint in your glasses it is important that people can see the eyes and make eye contact with you. Too much tint gives off the feeling that the person is hiding.
- A rule for frames is that they should be as wide as the widest part of your face and be in proportion to shape and size of your face.
- Some studies have shown that writing with red ink for long periods of time show that red on white can cause eyestrain and headaches.
- When selecting eyeglasses, look at them not only in the counter mirror, but also full length mirror. It is important to appraise the way glasses affect your overall silhouette.
- If you do not want to wear glasses and you can see distance but have trouble reading, one alternative is to wear one contact for reading in one eye. If you need to you can also wear a contact in the other eye for distance. This takes some getting used to but I find it

EYES

- Sometimes one of the things that we neglect are our eyes. Relaxation and circulation are some basic things that add to our eye health along with proper nutrition.
- Sometimes eye exercises can help to strengthen the eye muscles such as placing the head against the wall to assure that you do not move your head and look high at one corner of the room and then move eyes slowly from one corner to the other left to right and then right to left.
- Coffee, tea, and smoking all constrict the blood vessels.
- Vitamins B, C, and A are all essential to good eye health.
- Many people think that crows feet that develop around the eyes are hereditary but you do not have to have them. They are usually the result of poor vision habits, squinting, and neglect of the skin in the eye area.
- The skin around the eyes needs some special pampering with rich eye creams or moisturizers at night or when ever you are out in the sun for a long time. Do not rub it in put pat around the eye gently from outer corner of the eye to the inner corner.
- It would be good to wear a brimmed hat that shades your eyes or dark glasses to keep from squinting when you are in the sun.
- Take periodic eye breaks when your eye muscles get tired. Try shifting the focus of your gaze to distant object around the room for a few seconds. Open and close the eyes for four or five times very rapidly. Take stock of the lighting that is in your home or office to see if it may be too bright or too dull.
- When purchasing sunglasses, look for a better pair of lenses because inexpensive sunglasses often have inferior lenses full of irregularities that may interfere with clear vision.

HATS

- When wearing a hat remember proportion so that if you are small the hat doesn't overpower you.

- Hats are not worn as much now but always add a finishing fashion touch to an already elegant outfit.
- There are hats of every shape and color but some of the most interesting looks are the classic menswear, safari look, the pillbox, and the large oversized wide brims and fuller crowns.
- Many hats should be worn low on the brow and to the side. Women many times make the mistake of wearing a hat too far on the back of the head and lose the best look.
- If you are a small woman do not purchase too large a hat and let it wear you instead of you wearing the hat. Think proportion with this accessory.
- Straw hats are great for spring but if you have a limited wardrobe budget then purchase a felt hat which can be worn year round.
- Don't forget the turbans and fancy evening hats.
- The right hat adds height and credibility to the wearer. For a man or a woman, a hat has served as a traditional symbol of power, position, and authority.
- A woman's hat serves two main functions. It decorates a woman and also adds to her sense of presence.
- In testing successfully for hats in business, the medium brimmed hat and the women's medium sized fedora tested very well.
- The fedora should not look masculine so a little feather in it would add a more feminine look.
- It is fun to buy a classic cheaper hat and remove the trim on it and by taking it off you can add a band of trim from the material of your dress. Presto, a nice coordinated look.
- Hats can be worn at official receptions and luncheons, in restaurants, when shopping, church, or for virtually any occasion that takes place during the day.
- The only time it is necessary to remove your hat is when you are attending a movie, concert or theater performance. Take your hat off when the lights go down to avoid obstructing the view of the people behind you.
- Hats need to be treated with respect so always handle your hat gently and delicately place it in a hatbox for storage.
- With the exception of pillbox hats, they are rarely worn on the back of the head. It is best to adjust up or down on the forehead. A forward tilt to the middle of the forehead is best.
- When buying a hat, be sure to try it on in front of a full length mirror to take into consideration your own proportions.
- One of the reasons that women have a hard time wearing hats is because they do make a strong statement and they cause people to look at you the minute you walk into a room. Many women do not like this extra attention but most of the time the comments about the women wearing the hat is very positive.
- Felt is a year round fabric for hats and straw and linen are more for the spring and summer months.
- Feathers, fur and velvet are best for the winter months with velvet used mainly in the evening.

GENERAL TIPS

- If you have accidently washed a wool garment in water that is too hot, soak it in tepid water with a couple of capfuls of good shampoo to soften the wool and then reshape and block.
- Layering in your clothing can really be a good way to help proportion a figure. A vest, jacket, sweater and a shawl all draw interest and give flair to an outfit. They can disguise but at the same time completes an outfit and they give it more importance and a pulled together look.
- When we do not feel good about the way we look then we draw attention to our figure flaws by self consciousness in posture and awkwardness, so learn all about your figure and learn to dress in a manner that makes you feel good so you can put your best foot forward.
- A bargain no matter how little you paid for it is no bargain if you never wear it
- Rub a fresh fabric softener sheet over your slip and stockings to prevent dresses from clinging.
- If a zipper in your slacks or skirt gets stuck, try rubbing the point of a lead pencil over it. You can rub a cake of soap across the face of a plastic zipper for the same results.
- Dab transparent nail polish on the centers of sewed on buttons. This seals the thread and prevents unraveling.
- Learn to change the look of some of your older clothes by adding a new fashionable button.
- There are many ways that you can get contrast in an outfit such as adding collar and cuffs and use some creative fabric combinations such contrasting fabric and luster in the material.
- No matter how elegant and beautiful an outfit is you will not feel confident in it if it is not appropriate for the occasion. Take the time to find out from your hostess what kind of dress or ensemble to wear.
- Psychologists say that if someone does not care about their dress, it will enhance the negative feelings about themselves. Clothing is not the most important thing in the world because everything has its place, but it has been said that when we are well dressed we have a calmer feeling about ourselves and surroundings.
- It is important to not only purchase fashion magazines, and I prefer the fashion magazine pattern books, to get an idea of the new fashion trends but it is important to read the magazine and not just look at the pictures. You can get an idea of the shoes and shoe color, hair styles, accessories, length of hems etc. by being very observant.
- If your pants have bell bottoms then they should be appropriately taken in as well as the wide lapels on jackets or blouses. Skimpy shoulders can be padded and skirts can be shortened. Sometimes however, the alterations are not even worth it and ruins the shape.
- To help eliminate static cling when you do not have a spray handy try running a wire coat hanger between your dress and your slip to draw out the static electricity.
- Another way to eliminate cling is to starch your slips.

- Another static cling tip — if you will hang what you are planning to wear in the bathroom while you take a shower the steam will go into the fabric and eliminate static.
- Get rid of the ugly piling that some sweaters get by laying the fabric on a hard surface and light shave the garment with a razor. Be sure the fabric is dry and shave with the grain of the fabric.
- Rub white vinegar onto underarm perspiration stains with a white cloth and wash as usual. This is a good way to take stain and odor out.

FULL-FIGURED FASHION TIPS

- To get a clear view of your problem areas, take pictures of yourself in some of your most worn outfits, front, back and side view and it will help you develop a critical eye for what flatters from angles you usually do not see.
- Too tight an outfit makes you look heavier and very uncomfortable.
- Ease over your figure problem areas by not defining them such as a snug fitting sweater which will call attention to a full or small chest. An easy fitting top with a jacket makes the problem less noticeable.
- The oversized jackets are great to hide some figure flaws.
- If you have a hip problem, be sure the jacket you buy is below the largest part of your hip.
- To look thinner, choose a shawl collar or v neckline. This creates an illusion of length.
- Wear the chemise and dropped waist which is very good to extend a slim look.
- Avoid too much trim or if you do have trim on a garment be sure that it is vertical.
- Do not add bulk to an outfit. Wear sleeveless blouses under jackets.
- Do not wear wide belts that fit tightly around the waist or wear no belt or wear a narrow matching belt.
- Wear solid colors or one with a small design but be careful of the larger prints. They add width.
- Choose softly tailored skirts.
- Choose straight but loosely fitting and straight legged style slacks.
- Stay away from clinging fabrics and bright patterns.
- If you have legs that need to look thinner, then wear a neutral stocking with out any design or coordinate the color of your shoes to your hosiery which of course is coordinated with your dress.
- Shawl collars, A Line, Empire waistline, and V necklines create the illusion of length.
- Wear clothes that fit. Not too tight and not too large and it will automatically make you appear thinner.
- The full figured woman's clothing needs to fit perfectly, especially through the shoulders.
- Keep a touch of color at the face and a great hairstyle so the attention is focused on your face away from the figure.
- Thick waistlines can wear slacks but keep them dark and solid in color which are more slimming and combine them with a v neckline vest which will minimize your waistline.

- A long look illusion can also be achieved by wearing pants and jackets in matching colors.
- Keep your pants with a sharp pressed pleat.
- Many do not realize the importance of line in dressing. Line can make you look taller and slimmer, shorter or heavier.
- Do not wear oversized collars, cuffs and wide shoulder pads that will add width to a figure as well as horizontal lines.
- Do not wear two color outfits.
- Be aware that some vertical strips can add width if they are too wide and are the same width across the body.
- Some of the prints that they make up in clothes would look better in wallpaper than on a body, so be aware of what it will do in line to your body.
- A pants outfit can be an advantage in camouflaging large hips. Wear a loose third layer over pants. It is a matter of knowing the type of pant and how to use lines to camouflage.
- Coordinate the color of your shoes to your stockings which of course are coordinated with the color of your dress and you will look thinner.
- Soft pleating in the front of pants or a skirt can help hide the tummy bulge.
- Do not wear too tight a fit in a jean and be sure that you look from all angles in a full length mirror because some women's thighs are not even noticeable until she puts on a pair of jeans.
- Don't camouflage problem areas with a dull outfit but add attractive accessories at the neckline or add an attractive blouse.
- If you have bow legs, wear skirts a little longer and a soft fuller skirt rather than a straight line.
- An erect and correct posture can help several figure problems and make you look your best.
- Choose a vertical line rather than horizontal lines
- Use narrow self belts or no belt at all.
- Two piece outfits in one color or blended colors can add height and slim.
- Use colors that are decending or darker and duller. Shiny colors emphasize.
- Shape with lines and darts.
- When you use patterns, use subtle patterns and designs in clothes.
- Make good use of jackets that come over the hip as well as the over tops and make sure they cover the largest part of the hipline.
- Add vest accents.
- The v neckline will add a slimming vertical line.
- Avoid too bright a pattern or print or very small and very large prints.
- Avoid too small accessories.
- Avoid the mannish styles.
- Avoid too high hair dos or peeled hairdos. A too small head on a larger body does not create an attractive proportion.

- Sometimes two or more problems may contradict one another. If that happens, then dress for the problem that is most prominent.
- If you are heavy or big boned, avoid skintight clothes or large tent like garments because neither is going to make you look smaller.
- Choose loose clothes with tops that fall from the shoulder and give the illusion of softness and length.
- The best lines for a slimmer illusion are lines of softness and fabric that flows.
- For the full figure, well made clothes are a must so spend a little more and get quality instead of quantity.
- If you do not like the size of your backside, then do not buy pants with large back pockets..
- Choose hip length vests and jackets.
- Do not try to hide under a heavy winter coat with bulky fabric because the wrong coat style often exaggerates the parts of the figure we do not want to emphasize.
- If you have larger hips look for a loser body slimming coat. If you will have a slightly padded shoulder line then the bigger and broader silhouette at the top will draw the eyes up and away from the hip area.
- A stand up collar also focuses attention upward and frames a pretty face.
- Use vertical details such as set in pockets and high armholes to help create a more slender look.
- If you have a large bustline be careful of pockets over the bustline.
- It is best to avoid the boxy look of an untailored coat. Select a soft draping good quality wool.
- The pleating on a coat should begin near the shoulder line so that it does not draw attention to the hips by making that a focal point.
- If you have extra pounds then forget about the heavy down or quilted coats. They look good on the ski slopes but in general they make even the slimmest people look heavier.
- Be careful of too short a coat because it gives the upper body an oversized appearance and will accentuate problem hips and thighs.
- Other things to avoid until those added pounds are off are an oversized collar and broad lapels.
- In general avoid bulkiness.
- Horizontal quilting has a widening effect.
- The patch pockets are not good because they add padding to the hipline.
- Do not choose coats with elbow patches and cuffed sleeves because they add extra thickness and make the arms look heavier.
- If you have a heavy bustline, a wrap style coat can be very good for you.
- Do not wear pockets over a large bustline.
- A v neckline closure coat is best because it will elongate the neckline.
- A collarless or a coat without a lapel is good because it eliminates one more layer of fabric where you do not need it.
- Avoid large shoulder pads, shoulder pleating, and puffed sleeves.

- If you choose a belt, be sure it is narrow to eliminate a bulky constricted look.
- Do not wear two color outfits.
- Be aware that some vertical strips can add width if they are too wide and are the same width across the body.
- Some of the prints that they make up in clothes would look better in wallpaper than on a body, so be aware of what it will do in line to your body.

COATS — FULL FIGURED

- A slimming line in a coat fabric is a small vertical stripe or small print such as a herringbone or tweed.
- To look taller and slimmer choose a line in the coat that goes to the knee or slightly longer.
- A basic and neutral color is best so that it will go with all the clothes in your closet.
- Use color to emphasize with the lighter color expanding and the darker colors dimishing. By dark it does not mean only black, navy or dark brown but could mean maroon or dark purple etc.
- If you have any figure problems, then draw attention to your face with scarves, earrings and the right colors.
- If you have a large clothing budget then you can add some coats in different colors to extend the wardrobe.
- Don't forget to add some fashion touches to your coat such as a beautiful muffler or bright colors in scarves and if your figure is tall add a shawl.
- Too much fullness in a long sleeve should be avoided by the people who have broad hips or who are too short.
- Analyze your wardrobe for color. Black may be basic for some but perhaps your basics are beiges or navys. A coat in your best basic color then would be best. Remember that the darker colors will dimish the size of the figure where the lighter and brighter colors call attention to a figure and make things look larger.
- When buying a coat think about your profession. For instance if you work in an office, a more business like look in a coat may be best but if you spend most of your time at home with children then perhaps a tweed more sporty look would be best.
- If you travel or drive around a lot then consider a coat that is easy to get in and out of a car.
- If you have hip problems then you would not want a coat that hugs the hipline, a wrapcoat, or anything that ties at the waist.
- If you are short then the simple shape with a minimum amount of detail are best.
- Do not choose a raglan sleeve that will add a top heavy look.
- If you have a short neck and are large on top look for neat open collars and choose a coat that closes high on the neck.
- Don't forget that coats look attractive with accessories such as mufflers, scarves and pins.
- Do not wear oversized collars, cuffs and wide shoulder pads that will add width to a figure as well as horizontal lines.

THICK WAIST

- If you have a thick waist avoid a belted waist.
- If your hips can take this look, wear a low slung double wrap belt over the hipline and it will draw attention from the waist.
- A thick waist should avoid big dramatic buckles and wide cinch belts.
- Some good purchases for a thick waist would be empire waistline, unfitted A line over blouses, and a loose jacket.
- Tunics and the chemise are a good look also.
- Draw attention from the waistline with pearls or jewelry. Thicker waistlines should wear belts of the same fabric and color or no belt at all..
- Empire waistline, tunics, an unfitted a line, and a chemise look is good for a large waistline.

TUMMY BULGE

- If you have a tummy bulge then draw the eye upward.
- If you must wear a belt then keep it simple, toned to your outfit and never too tight.
- Empire waistline is also good for the tummy bulge as well as vests, overblouses, tunics, and jackets.
- Avoid pants and skirts that are too form fitting both in material and style.
- Soft pleating over the abdomen is better than a perfectly flat look which does not conceal at all.
- The tummy bulge can be concealed with overblouses, tunics, empire waistlines, boxy jackets and vests.
- Avoid tight fitting skirts and pants but choose small soft pleating.
- Hip hugging pants are not good for someone with a tummy bulge.

HEAVY LEGS

- Heavy legs look best in sheer dark hose that are color keyed to your outfit.
- You can wear skin colored hose and neutral shoes like bone or taupe or gray.
- For heavy legs, it is best to choose a classic shoe like a pump or sling back but nothing with a strap at the ankle or instep.
- Heels are best in a medium height and not too narrow.

SHORT WOMEN

- There are 37 million or more American women that are under 5-foot-4 and many get very frustrated at the current state of fashion which really seem to dictate to the taller woman. Short woman are constantly hearing rules of what not to do and what to do and sometimes it is so limiting and frustrating that they end up with the same type of clothing and look day after day.
- Be sure that your posture is good by standing and sitting tall and straight for this forms the basis for an attractive appearance.
- Create an illusion of height with vertical line in your wardrobe.

- The experts say that the best look is to have about l/3 proportion on top to 2/3 proportion on the bottom.
- Vertical line can be added with seams, buttons, trim or even with a v neckline as well as wearing the one color look or at least keep it blended in tone
- Short women are bombarded with rules about dressing in one long line or color to look taller and slimmer and sometimes this is so limiting that fashion for them becomes very boring. Obviously, a bold highly contrasting color combination is going to make you look shorter but many times blending the colors and even a low contrast combination may take some boredom out of your wardrobe.
- Small proportions are important in the patterns chosen but consider wearing some classic patterns such as tweeds in multicolors, some small herringbone looks, small polka dots and some great looks are to be found in paisleys and small stripes.
- If you want to wear layers without looking bulky then choose some of the lighter weight fabrics like silks and soft wool jersey.
- Do not wear an exaggerated dolmen sleeve or batwing sleeve. When this sleeve flares from the waistline it will shorten further. However choose a scaled down version of the batwing sleeve and have it start just below the bustline keeping a defined waist.
- Use a simple neckline with some interest added to make the eye come to the top of your body.
- Interest details at the shoulders is another good way to create a longer line.
- A shorter waisted woman will look best in a narrow belt that is the same color as garment she is wearing or subtle contrast. If you are long waisted your belt can be wider but never so wide that will make your legs look shorter.
- Shawl collars will make you look taller by bringing the eye to the top.
- The set in sleeve and v neckline are two lines that are least shortening.
- The rule for looking taller is for you to keep the fashion simple and uncluttered.
- The softly gathered or dirndl skirt is a nice line for women who are short to wear if the waistband is not too wide and the fabric is not too bulky. Choose a fabric that is soft and flow nicely such a s challis or silk.
- Pants that have a drawstring should be loose and never too full or overgathered and if you wear them tapered or medium straight in the leg it will be better than too full a leg.
- The blouson jacket should be more narrow with controlled fullness on top and should nave a slim not full or puffy sleeve.
- It would be better not to have a strong two color combination to create a shortening line such as a white blouse and black skirt.
- It is best for the short woman not to use too many contrasting colors to accessorize.
- There are always so many different changes in fashion as the seasons come and go but an important rule to remember when picking a new look is to dress to your own scale and proportion. Sometimes the new fashion can be very overwhelming to a short person but you can still wear it if you scale it down to your size — same fashion but less of it.

- Simply by shifting the center of interest in an outfit and placing the emphasis on other areas, you can then fool the eye of the observer by balancing the design lines of your garment to the best outlines of your figure. For instance if you are shorter you can give a strong impression of being taller by choosing a straight silhouette with the long look.
- Always look in a full length mirror and your eye will let you know immediately if you are in balance with the fashion you are wearing
- Dark colors are more slimming and elongate the figure where bright and light colors tend to enlarge and attract the eye. To look longer or taller wear a solid color from head to toe rather than patterns or prints. If you get too bored with that keep it blended or you could choose a small and subtle color with a small all over pattern.
- Tone your stockings to shoes not to the skirt color for this will give the illusion of a longer leg.
- Wear slimmer shapes in skirts and coats rather than the full or broad ones.
- Avoid the large collars or overly wide shoulders.
- Choose narrow rather than wide trousers and remember that slim does not necessarily mean tight or skinny. It simply means clothes that skim the body easily with out clinging or a soft flow of fabric with no constriction.
- The thinner the fabric such as jersey or soft wool the more gracefully it will fall.
- A tiny bit of shoulder padding will give a lift to your height and make you look longer.
- A good thing to remember is that lengthening or shortening a skirt or top even by l/4" can make all the difference in the proportions that are right for you.
- For the long slim look, begin at the top by lengthening
- your neckline with standup collars etc. Light attracts the eye and keeps the attention of the observer up higher so if you want to look taller or keep attention off of the hip and waist area wear something lighter toward the neck.
- It is best to wear belts that are color keyed to your outfits and not in bold contrast unless you have a small waist.
- Shoulders that are puffed can add height.
- Be cautious of largely padded shoulders which will only add volume and width instead of height.
- To look taller, colors that are the same from bottom to top are best but that gets rather boring so wear clothing in the same color family also.
- Avoid high contrast colors that meet at the waist or below.
- Complete your outfits with attractive accessories but wear them mainly at the neck level or higher.
- Earrings also keep attention focused high as do flattering hair styles and makeup.
- Soft graceful fabric is an ideal way to look taller because heavy fabric and bold designs can over power you.
- Drop shoulder styles work well when they are out of a soft unlined fabric.
- Cuffed trouser, ankle strap shoes, ankle bracelets, contrasting border hems, horizontal stripes at hems and midcalf length pants and skirts will shorten a person.

- Be careful not to bring undo attention to your legs so stay away from color contrast between your stockings and skirt.
- If you are short and heavier do not wear heavily textured hosiery.
- Open or v vamp shoes and pumps are great for making your legs look longer as they create an unbroken line.
- A good dress for someone who wants to look slimmer and taller is the clean line chemise. It has no belt, just soft straight fluid flow from shoulder to hem. This is great for the woman with waist and hip problems because the line bypasses those areas with a clean line.
- If you keep your shoes, hose and color of a straight line dress in one color or blends it will make you look much taller.
- If you want leg length, the general rule is always keep the darker tones on the bottoms and the lighter tones on the top.
- Don't cut yourself in half with color as with a light top, and dark bottom especially if you are short. It is better to add a slimming piece like a long knit vest, a jacket or even a cardigan.
- If you want to use color to look taller, then put the lighter or brightest color toward the neckline so that the eye will travel upward to create a longer line
- If you are a small person, be careful to not get too bold a print to overpower you.

TALL WOMEN

- Most of the time the tall woman should just enjoy her height and look good in the high fashion of the season. The basis for the tall woman to look attractive is good posture which seems to be a problem for some women in this category. It does not matter how wonderful an outfit that a tall woman wears, if she has a slumped rounded shoulder posture the fashion loses its look.
- Tall is at least 5'6" or taller. Because of your height you can wear many details such as ruffles, big buttons, pleats, gathers and large cowl collars. You have the height to show off details without looking cluttered or overwhelmed by them.
- Some of the more noted taller women are Princess Diana, Cheryl Tiegs, Lynda Carter, and Brooke Shields, so if you are tall you are in good company.
- The taller woman has a greater number of options in the creation of line. Height is an automatic asset for the taller woman and shows clothing to the best advantage.
- One problems that a tall woman finds is that the ready to wear sizes do not fit because the sleeves are too short, pants and skirts are too short or waistline is in the wrong spot. If this is your problem. then shop around for a certain brand name that will meet these problems and stick with that brand.
- When things need to be altered, do not buy them if they have to be altered too much. They lose the general look they were designed to create.
- The perfectly proportioned tall figure has a hipline that falls at l/2 the total height and knees that fall at l/4 the total height.
- If you are tall and perfectly proportioned, you can wear strong horizontal lines, cropped pants, broad shoulder styles, wide belts and long jackets.

- If you are long legged you could wear a dropped waisted dress, overblouse or jacket which is hip length or longer and a skirt hem up to the knee or mid knee to break the long legged look.
- Have a lot of fun with color when you are tall by wearing layers of contrasting separates.
- Bold prints are good possibilities and make the most of the spectacular border prints, big scarf prints and vivid Hawaiian screen prints.
- Big plaids are also good as well as wide stripes. This is for the slim tall woman with good proportions.
- Even if you prefer not to draw attention to your waist have fun with big interesting buckles.
- The taller slender woman can wear a greater number of accessories than a woman of lesser stature.
- Use accessories to focus attention on some of your best features.
- Hats are a wonderful accessory on the taller woman and frame the face beautifully.
- Lace Jabots and large shawls and scarves are some effective looks.
- Jewelry can be used in large amounts by the taller woman so use dramatic jewelry to create a super look that cannot be worn by all women.
- Consider layering your jewelry and use scarves with jewelry.
- Use the larger handbags for a great finishing touch to any outfit.
- You can shorten the upper part of your figure by wearing short jackets or wide belts.

THIN WOMEN

- It is interesting to me that most women no matter how slim they are never feel that are thin enough. This can be a real obsession to some women because this society puts a real emphasis on the model thin figure. However, there are a few people whose metabolism or genes is geared to being thin.
- It has been said that you can never be too rich or too thin but you can be too thin at least for some styles of clothing.
- If you are bony in certain areas then stay away from straight skirts or skin tight jeans.
- Tops should have soft full lines.
- Halters, low necklines, bare midriffs and short shorts will all emphasize thinness.
- Wear full cut clothing to fill out the curves of your body.
- Use textured fabrics.
- Almost all clothes look better when they are draped on a slender figure.
- To add some roundness to areas wear fabrics such as terry cloth, cable knits and some soft wools.
- Add shoulder pads to some loose fitting jackets, blazers, pull over sweaters and cardigans.
- Tuck your sweaters into your skirts and slacks to make your body look rounder and hips appear flatter and smoother.
- Choose blouses with smocking, large collars and puffed sleeves to create the illusion of roundness.

- Dress in the layering look with vests, blouses and sweaters, dusters, and jackets.
- Wear wide contrasting belts and cummerbunds.
- Jackets that stop at the waist with contrasting pants would be an interesting look for someone thin.
- Experiment with accessories such as scarves tied in big floppy bows around your neck.
- Avoid high hairdos and high hats if you are short and thin.
- Pants of all types look great on the tall, slender figure.
- To add fullness at the hips, try pants that are pleated at the waistline.
- If you are thin with no hips, wear skirts with graceful fullness and things that soften the line of the hip like loose overshirts or an open shirt jacket and softly gathered slacks.

SKINNY LEGS

- Textured hosiery and knit hose are very good for the thin leg.
- Herringbone and diamond patterns are good for day time wear, lacy designs for night.
- Contrasting hosiery will make the leg look larger.
- The classic taupe and suntan does not call attention to a leg whether too large or too small.

PROPORTION AND LINE

- Many women today go shopping with any idea of what their proportions are (where they are long and short) and therefore many clothes end up in their wardrobe without being worn because of what they do to a figure.
- Be aware that lines are very deceiving and can take inches off or add height. Therefore, vertical adds height and slims while horizontal shortens and adds width. This can be accomplished with seams or prints in fabric.
- Proportion is a major design element that is a must in considering a purchase. Most clothes today are beautiful in design but we have to ask ourselves, for whom because each person's body has a slightly different set of proportions.
- Even if you happen to be the same weight and height of someone else, the chances are that your proportions are not the same. — therefore the design for one woman might be perfect for her but totally wrong for another.
- Most of us do not have perfect proportions and so we need to look for clothes and accessories that are harmonious with our body structure. If you have ever bought something because it looked great on a good friend or even a model in a magazine perhaps you found out that it can be very costly when you do not think about your own proportions and body structure.
- Proportion is very simple and essentially what it means is that you make one sections of your body look longer, more narrow, wider, larger or smaller, or shorter. A good example would be to wear a high waist band either in slacks or skirt and this will make your legs appear longer and the upper portion of you will appear shorter.

- If you use a blouse or jacket with shoulder pads then because you look wider on top it will make you hips look more narrow Just remember that lines are very deceiving and by cleverly using line and color you can emphasize your most positive features and play down your negative ones..
- Think about collars and lapels when you are purchasing a dress, suit of coat. They should be scaled to your height and your size..
- Examine the lines of the collar to determine what they will do to your shoulder width.
- Collars which point down can narrow the should and the large shawl collars which drape too much can shorten the legs and look out of date.
- A standard notched collar can be worn by all body types.
- The important thing to learn is that the correct lines discussed here and color can give an unbalanced look if used incorrectly, so examine your figure, your good and bad points and start using the knowledge to dress correctly. Lines in clothing are very important considerations because they carry the eye in a certain direction and will emphasize certain areas of our bodies..
- Some lines you should consider are seams, weaves of fabric, details , and necklines.
- The eye follows the line so if the line is horizontal it will widen, if it vertical it will slim and add height.
- Don't forget details such as border prints ruffles, piping, buttons, and anything similar that carries the eye horizontal or vertically is considered a line.
- One of the areas that we sometimes do not consider that may emphasize or repeat a line is the neckline of our clothes. Any line that you do not wish to emphasize in your face, do not repeat such a square jaw do not wear a square collar.
- The length of a skirt or dress depends on how you feel when you see yourself standing and sitting in a full length mirror. Usually the best length is I to I/2" below the heaviest part of the leg.
- A planned focal point should be in your dress every day such as earrings or makeup or a ruffled neck blouse can move the focus to your face. A skirt with a slit or a high heeled shoe can place the focal point at your leg.
- Do not put all your focus on a good feature if you expose a poor feature such as wearing a dainty shoe on small feet if it will make you look out of proportion if you have extra weight.
- Use focal points to draw attention away from figure flaws. Jewelry when used against a dark dress can draw attention away from the figure. and jewelry against a light background will call attention to your figure.
- A lapel that is too wide or too narrow will not dated as quickly as one that is medium width and will stay in fashion longer. If you think about the clothes that you have now and how wide or extremely narrow lapels date the purchase of that piece of clothing. Save some money and think basic.
- Think about the yokes that are in clothing that you buy because a yoke that has gathers will have a softening effect on broad shoulders and yet it can have a great balancing effect on narrow shoulders.
- Soft gathers below a yoke can balance and camouflage a full bust if it is not too bulky.

- Soft gathers can also be used to make a small bust not as obvious.
- To make the shoulder look broader use the wider and more shallow neckline, the wider collar and lapel.
- Yokes, jewelry and scarves and also horizontal top stitching, and shoulder pads are all helpful to the narrow shoulder.
- To make the shoulder look more narrow, use some center interest such as longer necklaces, buttons, scarves, more narrow and deeper necklines, inset sleeves, and narrow lapels.
- The set in sleeve is good on all body types and gives a balanced look to the body.
- Only the well proportioned individual should wear a sleeveless garment or halter neckline. A halter neckline will make a broad shoulder look much larger and a narrow shoulder much smaller, just the opposite effect that you want.
- A longer jacket will make the legs appear shorter while a short jacket will add length to the legs.
- Always consider texture of material — for instance, a cable knit sweater will add width to the upper body more than one that is a lighter weight.
- One good way to train your eye regarding proportion and what it does is to study the store windows, fashion magazines as well as people on the street and try to figure out why a particular outfit looks balanced or unbalanced.
- Consider these items in determining what is best for you: color, details, widths and length, textures, and basic line of the outfit. With an awareness and putting it into practice, you will find that you can shop easier and put details together for you that are a well balanced fashion look.
- Horizontal lines of course, emphasize width especially when they are repetitive but you can create an impression of length on the body if you will place it above or below the middle of your body and then it will make one or the other section look longer. An example of this is a dropped waist dress — this lengthens the upper body. However, a strong horizontal line in a place you do not want to emphasize such as your hips should be considered.
- A strong single vertical line will give the greatest impression of height.
- Curved lines such as a soft draped look will do the same thing as straight line and hide many figure flaws. They emphasize the curves of the body and make a soft and more feminine look.

NECKLINES

- With all the beautiful accessories out today that adorn the neckline, it is important for you to know how to make the best of your neckline beauty.
- If you have what we call the dowager's hump at the base of the neck, then collars that are set away from the neck in the back are more flattering.
- If you have a thick short neck it will look more in proportion if you wear a collar set away from the neck all around not a crew or turtle neck that hugs close to the body.
- Long thin necks will look better in higher collars and can wear choker necklaces.

- In choosing a proper neckline in a garment, consider the width of your shoulders and balance the shoulders with the width of your hips, length of your neck, and the shape of your face.
- Consider the hairstyle that is best for your face and if your neck is not one of your best features you can camouflage with fashions and proper hairstyle.
- A softly tied blouse is a good way to hide lines that are on the neck.
- A scarf that is tucked into a neckline and some colorful beads that hang low will draw attention away from the neck.
- Another popular look is a ruffled collar to hide neck wrinkles and add a touch of fashion with the popular cameo pin.
- If you do not know if you have a long or short neck, draw an outline of the head, neck and shoulders on your mirror with some lipstick or a bar of soap. You will be able to see your proportions clearly. You can do this also to determine what face shape you have.
- A long neck is usually an asset and most of the top models have this feature. But if you have one that is exceptionally long and thin, try to create an illusion of fullness at your neckline with your hairstyle.
- A jewel neckline is an unfinished neckline that you can add accessories and designs to such as buttons, top stiching, scarves, etc. The jewel neckline is a very simple look. If you have a bony neck, it will not look the best on you without some softness added.
- If you have a long neck, a dowager's hump, or poor posture, you will need help when wearing a neckline with no collar. Use scarves, jewelry or an extra lay on collar to achieve some balance and it will also camouflage.
- A narrow collar that stands up can be worn by most figure types and also most people can wear a mock turtleneck unless your neck is extremely short or perhaps heavy.
- A turtleneck is best on the medium to long neck.
- Be creative with jewelry working with beads in all shapes, sizes, colors, and lengths. You will find that jewelry can spark up a dull and drab outfit like almost nothing else can.More women can wear the softer type of fabric rather than heavier look at the neckline.
- The mandarin collar oriental type lok is an attractive neckline for most people except the very short necked person.
- Bows that are tied at the neckline create a softness around the face. Soft fabric will fall softly without too much bulk.
- Practice tying your bows so that they are not lopsided and are attractive.
- If you have a long neck you might try wrapping the ties around the neck for a sophisticated look instead of typing them in a bow.

FABRICS

- Never underestimate the importance of a good fabric. Everyone loves the feel of a soft fabric in clothes to a rough and itchy one and a beautiful fabric makes the person who is wearing it feel good.

- The look and feel of silk is a very useable and versatile fabric and is great for blouses.
- Be careful that you do not get too much polyester mix in a blouse or it will not feel as soft or look as luxurious.
- Educate your fingertips to the feel of a fine fabric and an inferior one. A god material should feel soft, and luxurious. The better it feels, the better it probably is. The finest weaves feel very soft.
- A good wool does not wrinkle very easily.
- To save some money, look for some of the modern synthetic blends that resemble silk or elegant cottons.
- There are some polyester blends that feel and look exactly like silk, satin or a polished cotton and are much less expensive.
- Good fabrics are more expensive and do require more care that the poor quality ones.
- Good fabrics not only hang better and clean better, but look more elegant and will last longer Perhaps a few less items of clothing in the best of fabrics would be a better buy then more of the cheaper brand.
- Be careful about cleaning bills but some of the silks and finest fabrics can be washed perfectly well by hand. They should be washed in a cold water with a fine fabric soap such as Woolite.

CHAPTER 5

Genesis 37:3
"... gave him a special gift — a brightly colored coat." LB

PUT ON YOUR BEST COLOR

One of the best things that you can do for yourself is to find yourself a good color analyst in your area and find out your color key. This will save you money and time over and over again because you cannot even start to coordinate a wardrobe or purchase make up with out knowing your proper color key. When you know what colors are best on you, it is much easier to put together a wardrobe that will extend and save you money. It takes the guesswork out of shopping and will save money in the long run because you do not have a mirage of various colors that do not go together to make a working wardrobe.

Every one of you are either cool in your skin tones or warm. Cool means that you will wear colors that have an absence of yellow or gold in the undertone. Warm means that the colors have a presence of yellow or gold tones in them. An example of this would be pink and peach. Pink is made by putting red and white together which will yield your pink shade but when you add yellow to that you will get varying shades of peach. Therefore pink is a cool color and peach is a warm color.

- A cool skinned person will have pink, sallow yellow, blue, or olive in the undertones of their skin. A warm skinned person will have peachy or golden tones.

- If you are in the cool category you will be further divided into Summer or Winter people. This means that you both will wear the absence of yellow in the undertone and the summers will be the softer pastels and the winters will wear the deeper colors. An example would be soft pink versus hot pink or a soft mauve color versus a deep burgundy.
- If you are in the warm category you will be divided into Springs and Autumns. The Spring people will wear colors that have the clear yellow undertones in them and the Autumn people will wear the muted yellow or gold undertones. An example would be a clear orange color for Spring and a muted rust for autumn. Both can wear orange and rust but the difference would be the depth of the color.
- I have found that most people have an instinct into what color looks best on them, cool or warm, but they are influenced by hubby, moms, peers and the fashion industry.
- What you have to determine is not if you like the color but if the color likes you.
- Everyone can wear a shade of red if it has the correct undertone, either absence or presence of yellow or gold tones. If is a cool red it will have blue under tones and the warm red would be the orangery reds.
- If you are wearing a color too deep or too light for your skin tone then balance it out with your makeup by either adding softer shades or deeper ones.
- Check out your wardrobe to determine what your color trend seems to be and then choose additions to go with these. If you know your color key, there will be no more guess work.
- The most mixable colors are those in the neutral families such as the blacks, browns, navys and grays. These may seem a little dull to you but they really are not when you add some of the beautiful bright colors, prints and paisleys with them.
- Many people just assume that brown goes with brown, black with black etc. but mix tones of different color families. You would not wear dark blue and dark brown together for the best look but you could put together two different color families in navy and beige using one dark and one lighter color.
- Do not throw out any clothes because they are not right for you in color but add accessories such as a scarf or blouse in your correct color so that it is close to your face and will be reflected as such. Gradually as you purchase new clothing you can discontinue using the incorrect colors. This process takes time.
- Do not take your color swatches that are best for you too literally. When you are matching fabric, it should be in the same color family but does not have to match exactly. This can be very frustrating when you have to match a color perfectly.
- Be aware that color can take us out of harmony. For instance if you wear the incorrect color even though the garment is correct, it can take you out of balance and you may not feel comfortable in the outfit and not even know why.
- If someone compliments you on the color of your blouse instead of commenting on how nice you look as a whole, then think if the color of the blouse may be wearing you instead of you wearing the blouse. In short all aspects of dressing should be seen as a harmonious blend.

- Black is not necessarily slimming because it many times creates too definite a silhouette. Medium to dark shades are sometimes much better.
- Keep in mind that the best colors alone will not make you look great in your clothes because it is important to consider how the color is being used such as whether you us a light or dark color and where you place it in your clothing. If you have the light color on a larger hipline it will emphasize your hips.
- Dark colors minimize the areas they cover whereas the brighter and lighter colors emphasize that area.
- If you are going to purchase a suit, the solid colors are best but tweeds and muted plaids work through a wardrobe very well.
- Navy, gray, and beige suits are great business colors in the executive position and worn with a white or bright blouse or shirt are very good for authority dressing.
- Purple, olive green, and gold are sometimes offensive. Avoid these colors in large items.
- It is best to buy clothing only after checking out the color in the daylight not artificial lights of the stores.
- It has been found that a businesswoman will not be taken seriously when wearing a pink suit.
- . The deep teals, emerald green, bright blue, and purple make a bright color statement on their own and should be in a superior fashion design and fabric.
- Unless you can afford a special set of accessories for each ensemble you wear, keep the neutrals predominant and then use the secondary colors for interest. An example would be a beige suit with a burgundy blouse would be fine with burgundy or black shoes but a burgundy suit with beige shoes would not be best because you would see shoe first since it is lighter than the suit.
- When mixing neutrals with a secondary color it is a good idea to keep the darker shade on the bottom. You could reverse the look but because the bottom half of us is proportionately larger, it is more difficult to keep a pleasing look of balance. An example would be a white blouse and black skirt would looks better than a white skirt and a black blouse.
- If you have the more gentle contrasts in your skin tone for instance a medium hair color and a medium skin tone then you will look best in the more gentle contrasting colors but if you have strong contrast in your hair and skin such as black hair and ivory skin then you can effectively wear much stronger contrasts in your colors.
- Some of the bright colors are very expressive and give off a positive aura such as the color red. It can be used to show strength and persuasiveness.
- Height is a very important consideration in choosing too much color because it can overwhelm or overshadow a small person, or on a tall person it can overwhelm the person looking at you.
- If you choose linen fabric for a suit, then it is best to choose a darker color because it will look slightly less wrinkled. Also a more coarse weave of linen will wrinkle less. Linen that has some blends in it may be better. Test the wrinkling by wadding the fabric in your hand.

- Many people do not think of color as an accessory but it really is and can be the most eye catching accessory that you wear.
- Some people say that they sometimes get compliments when they are not wearing their best color — however, many women have a knack for putting together an attractive look and the observer is actually complimenting you on what is being worn rather than the effect of the color upon the woman or man. Also, an observer may love a particular color or the outfit may be a very attractive style.
- Color is not an exact science so it is not whether you look horrible or great in a color but what is good, better, or best.
- Consider the color you put in your hair so that it matches the undertones in your skin. If yellow does not look good with your skin tone then too many golden highlights in hair will not look good either.
- Glass frames are another big consideration in choosing color. Not only should they blend with the coordination in our wardrobe but should complement our skin tones. See section on glasses.
- Many times the colors that we put in our home and try to live with for years can cost us money because after a short amount of time we are tired of the color. We seem to live better and more comfortable with colors in our color key.
- Color is one of the main reasons that we tire of something whether it is in our home or in our closet.
- Most women have a closet full of clothes in all the different color groups but there is no one who can wear colors from both undertones and all of the values and intensities and look equally good in them all.
- If you think back to those colors in which you have felt the best and in which you have received the most compliments, then you might have an idea or a good clue as to which colors are best for you.
- There are many ways to wear color but a good rule to follow is to use one accessory of intense color in an outfit and you will find that is generally enough.
- Many bright colors together in an outfit makes an entirely different fashion statement. If this is done properly however, it can have a very interesting fashion look.
- When wearing a white shoe for it to look the best wear it with a white outfit or with a predominantly white background, or soft pastels. If you wear white shoes with something too dark it will be the first thing that you see.
- Consider it a five year plan to eliminate the colors that are not best for you and gradually purchase into your own color key.
- Your best colors do not change as you grow older other than the colors you wear can soften with age but you will never be a warm skinned person if you were born cool.
- If you get a tan continue to stay in your color key but you can then wear some brighter colors. Its all a matter of balance.
- It is a hard task to try and coordinate a wardrobe without knowing your personal color key because people have a tendency to buy a multitude of colors both good and bad.

- Most of us have dressed all of our lives and never thought about the color we are putting on even though color can make us look healthy or ill, older or younger, and tired or refreshed.
- When you hear the word taupe referring to a good basic, the best way to describe it is that is gray brown. When you look at it you can see gray and you can see brown.
- Be careful of black because it is not necessarily slimming when it creates too definite a silhouette. Medium to dark colors may be better. Make use of full length mirrors to get an overall image.
- It has been recommended that a person wear a stimulating bright color when wishing to be chosen from a number of applicants to appear on a TV game show.
- Color has been considered to be the number one factor in attracting the customer to any product.
- My experience with color is that there are certain colors which are in harmony with each individual person and others which are not. There are a variety of factors which influence why we like or do not like a certain color.
- When you wear your own best color key you will feel more comfortable and the colors will make your skin appear smoother, clear and glowing
- The correct colors minimize lines and circles.
- The colors that a person wears for the day tell a lot about how they are feeling and thinking.
- Many women are very shy about color and stay in the same shades over and over again. When you know your color key, it helps you to step out with a variety of new colors to help perk up an otherwise dull wardrobe.
- Some people think that they can't wear certain colors but you can wear a hue of every color if it has the correct undertone. The exception being yellow. Some people do not look good in yellow at all. If there is too much sallow yellowness in the skin, yellow will turn the skin more yellow.
- It is fun to use the cool and warm colors together but in order to have a workable co-ordinated wardrobe, the majority of accessories should be in colors that coordinate well and move through your wardrobe easily. Its very hard to put a rust skirt with a pink blouse and have it look as good as pink with a burgundy skirt.
- An example of cool and warm colors together would be a skirt with yellow and orange accents on a blue background. If the background were mostly blue then this would be what would reflect the most of your skin and kept in mind when purchasing cool or warm.
- As a general rule, the brighter colors work best as accents except in play clothes, sports wear, and are beautiful in blouses, sweaters, and scarves.
- It has been said that color follows a pattern of the economic feeling in our society. When the times seem kind of depressed, then the color scheme seems to follow with the dull depressing colors such as gray etc.
- The studies show that colors seems to follow a cycle beginning with bright colors, then to pastels, then goes into basics such as black and white.

- If Africa is big in the news the color trends for the season may follow the ethnic prints or yellow and green. Interesting but who really knows.
- Achieve new looks in color by layering with two blouses in two different colors.
- One of the most flattering beauty tools you use is color and therefore should be given due respect in using it as part of our beauty regime. When used to our best advantage it will give you the most benefit.
- Do not pick a color that is too over powering for your skin tone because your face is your focal point and you do not want to detract from it.
- Scientists say that color is capable of affecting our moods, sensations, and even the way we will relate to the world. They have done tests to prove that color or the lack of it can affect our state of mind, reflexes, blood pressure, heart beat. and respiration rate. Different colors can depress us or excite us and even tranquilize us.
- Because of this information, color is being used much more effectively in offices, restaurants, hospitals and other businesses to achieve the proper affect on the client. That says that it is important to take color serious in our surroundings such as our home as well as our closet. Imagine if everything you looked at were gray.
- It is interesting to me to see the medical profession begin to use color in pediatrics to cheer the small patient by adding the bright warm colors to walls and also using the tranquil blues to help other types of patients relax more.
- If you are a very small person, use three shades of the same color or keep it very blended. This is called monochromatic use of color and will add height to a short figure.
- Pale shades give importance to a small figure.
- Color also affects many of our value judgments of people. On a first impression, a woman wearing a gray suit may be thought of as very conservative and businesslike while a woman that is wearing a bright red dress may be thought of as exciting, stimulating and very romantic.
- There is a lot of guess work going on to determine ones best color key but the only true way is to be color draped with cloths to see what they are doing to your skin tone. Be sure that you choose someone who knows what they are doing because there are a lot of wrongly color draped people out there.
- A person who wears the correct color but has too much intensity in the color will make the color look like it is wrong for her. One way to overcome this problem is to balance the color out with correct makeup. A person who does not wear makeup needs to be even more careful that she wears the right color.
- Everyone reacts whether consciously or not to the colors you are wearing. If you wear a lot of white they think of you as pure and fresh.
- When you wear all black you may be considered mysterious.
- The more subtle the colors and the color combinations that you choose the less aware people will be of the influence the colors have on them, but they are affected whether they are aware of it or not.

- Learn to use color with skill and you can take a moderately priced or even some of your old clothes and blend the colors so expertly that the final outfit will look much more rich than when worn in parts.
- Wearing variations in the same tone look very sophisticated and especially in the neutral tones like white, black and beige, or other varying shades of blues.
- The neutrals, beiges, tans, taupe, grays, black, whites and navy are key for coordination and the wide variety of shades and tones of these are fashion classics and good every year. They will never be unfashionable and they always appear elegant as well as being extremely versatile. They should constitute the framework of your wardrobe.
- If you have an olive complexion, then avoid any of the beige colors that have yellow undertones.
- The beige or taupe raincoat is the most professional color to lend status to your appearance.

COLOR PERCEPTIONS

- Red has the reputation of representing courage and suggests and extroverted and optimistic personality.
- Red is the color to wear when you want to draw attention to yourself because your eye will naturally seek out the brightest color in an audience.
- Red is also the color to wear when you are shopping if you want to be waited on promptly
- Red comes on strong and a little goes a long way.
- When wearing pink, you are thought of as little girl, nice but not smart in business.
- Mauve, pink's cousin continues the relaxed attributes of pink, but add stability.
- If you dislike pink, you are a no nonsense person wanting to know every detail.
- Orange is a great color when first seen but hard to accept for many people. It has been said that orange personalities give great parties, are constantly on the move looking for something new and change friends frequently.
- If you do not like orange many times you also dislike public kissing and hugging
- Orange brought little negative association but was considered cheerful and many of the extroverted people wear this color. The muddier shades of orange were not as well liked and were considered cheap such as rust
- Brown is earths stable color and people who like brown stay at home or at least in their own neighborhood. They are said to be frugal in their budgets and get the most out of their money.
- Green is natures color and is restful and non demanding. The experts say that the people who like green usually do not provoke arguments and go along with the crowd.
- Green is associated with tranquility but only some greens are peaceful. Others cause negative reactions in people like olive green.
- There has been some testing on green which says that it creates an air of suspicion about the honesty and integrity of the person. They say it is best to avoid wearing this color in the monies profession.

- Aqua is said to reflect good taste and judgment. Many people like aqua and many wear it well. Equal amount of green and blue mix to make aqua can be worn by everyone. The way to tell if aqua is on the cool or warm side is if it is more blue aqua then it is for the cool skin and if it is green aqua then it is best for the warm skins.
- Blue is said to calm and shows professionalism and they have found that blue can lower the blood pressure and ease anxiety.
- Navy or deep blue tells us that you are in command of a situation.
- Blue is associated with celestial things (probably because the sky is blue) and is associated with the spiritual side of things. Blue is a very restful color and is a good color for a bedroom. The statistics have shown also that blue kitchens cause people to eat less than ones in the bright warm shades such as yellow.
- Blue is a cool color and is sometimes associated with sadness and trust. It is really a favorite color for many people.
- Yellow is said to be a color that can be seen further than any other color. Therefore this is a good color for buses and road signs. It is also said that yellow is identified with the mind and the intellect.
- Yellow is a good mood lifting color and a good color to concentrate on for a few minutes if you are depressed.
- Yellow is a color that is said to show confidence and composure as well as caring and giving.
- Purple makes people think of high rank and prosperity.
- Our perception of color is often dependent on past associations and experiences.
- The research has found that the wrong colors in an office or factory can destroy employee morale and the right colors increase productivity.
- An interesting study was done in an airline. The interior of the plane was upholstered in yellow green and there was a marked increase in air sickness.
- It has been found that a room painted a certain shade of pink had a quieting effect on people who were agitated or violent.
- Here is an interesting thought for you. Why do you suppose fast food restaurants use the bright color combinations of yellow, orange, shocking pink and red. It makes us move faster and not linger over our food.

CHAPTER 6

Isaiah 60:5
"Then you will look and be radiant"
"Isaiah 60:5 NIV

GROOMING COMPLETES THE LOOK

One of the things that some women fail to take into consideration to look fashionable is the total look of grooming. Personal grooming is one of those things that is easy to overlook especially if your life is a very busy one, but there is no way to look fashionable and successful if your grooming is not up to snuff. Lets go over some of the infractions.

- Be sure that when you go out there is not dandruff on your collar. This is especially bad with dark colored clothes. Take a soft wet washcloth and brush the shoulder area before you step out.
- Take time to take care of your hands and nails. This is an area that some women have a tendency to forget and it takes away from the total look of grooming. The bitten down nail into the flesh is a very unattractive look.
- Panty hose with baggy knees and runs are to be avoided. It is a good idea to have an extra pair on hand in your handbag in case a run occurs.
- If you will buy at least two pair of the same color then when a run does occur you can cut off the leg of the one that has the run, and do the same with the extra pair when it

gets a run and then you will still have one good pair with extra support over the tummy.

- Be sure that you look in a full length mirror before going out so that you can see that no slip or lining are hanging below the hem or your garment. I do not care how carefully you are dressed, if these show it is poor grooming.
- Be sure the hem of your garment is sewn correctly and not pulled or puckered for that looks very messy.
- Be sure that the undergarment straps are not showing, or that they can be seen through sheer material. If straps are a problem, try sewing a small strap holder underneath especially on sleeveless dresses.
- Do not spend a lot of hard earned cash on trendy and faddish items for it is not being a good steward of your money. If you do, buy only one item for the season because in 6-8 months you will be tired of it.
- Patent leather will shine like new after a quick wipe with Windex.
- We are a very busy society and when our lives are so active some times these very basic grooming items do not get taken care of but I believe everyone wants to look as good as possible but it takes some planning and organization and awareness of the infractions..
- One grooming infraction might be unkempt or unwashed hair. Get a good hairdresser that can keep your hair in an easy style for you and give you some good helps in keeping it in place and shiny.
- Be sure that your clothes are always free of wrinkles and spots. You can have the most beautiful wardrobe but if it is not kept clean and pressed it will take on a sloppy face.
- Check all buttons to be sure that they are not hanging and that they all match.
- White blouses and shirts should be worn only once because of hair oil on the collar and dirt on the cuffs. To get this out try rubbing shampoo on the collar ring instead of using detergent..
- A daily bath should be taken. We live in a pretty polluted world and odors are easily detected in small working conditions. Perfume or cologne does not cover up a dirty body. It only smells like sweat mixed with perfume or cologne.
- Never forget your underarm deodorant.
- Be aware of your breath and keep breath mints on hand.Do not chew gum.
- Take good care of your teeth with regular visits to the dentist. Many breath problems come from rotting teeth and unhealthy gums.
- Your teeth should be brushed frequently and cleaned professionally to prevent yellowing.
- Your dress or suit may be beautiful but if it is soiled, snagged or stained it will not flatter you so treat your clothes to the best of care on a regular basis. This will not only improve your image but will increase the shelf life of your clothes.
- Every day before you go out examine your clothes for spots, split seams or missing buttons.
- Do not wear jewelry that will pull a thread on the fabric.

- Remove your shoes before stepping in and out of skirts and pants to prevent catching the hem with the heel or toe of your shoe.
- If you get dressed after you have put your make up on, take a scarf and hold one corner with your teeth. Then put it over the top of you hair and tie at the neck. The makeup will not get on your clothes when putting something over your head and also it will muss your hair less.
- If you put your makeup on after you get dressed, put on a dress shield or drape a towel over your shoulders to catch any flakes of the makeup.
- Be sure that you allow both deodorants and perfumes to dry thoroughly before putting your clothes on. These products can discolor or even weaken certain fabrics.
- If you get something on your clothing treat it as soon as possible. Rinse with water if the fabric is washable and the stain is water soluble.
- Be very careful with silk fabrics because in attempting to get out the stain, you can remove the color from the silk fabric.
- Keep a personal bottle of spot remover in a handy place for more difficult stains
- It is a good idea to test what you are using to remove a stain in an inconspicuous place perhaps in the under side of the hem before ruining the garment if it does not work.
- Do not carry sharp or heavy objects in your pockets because this can pull the fabric out of shape or even break the seams.
- Things that you carry in your pockets can wear out the linings more quickly so store those things in your handbag.
- Continually check your clothes for spots and repairs before you hang them up.
- Hang your dresses and blouses on padded hangers or the wider plastic hangers.
- When you hang your clothes make sure the shoulder seams hang straight and if you will fasten the buttons, hooks and zippers the clothing will remain more wrinkle free.
- If you say you do not have time to do all of these things, remember that it takes more time to make a repair due to careless clothing handling than to do it right in the first place.
- Before you put your sweaters away, turn them inside out and lay them over the back of a chair to be freshened, then store them loosely by folding and placing flat on a shelf or in a drawer. Do not hang sweaters.
- Personal grooming is essential to give you that final polished look. That means proper deodorant, clean hair and breath and no run down shoes.
- Be sure that your clothes are nicely pressed.
- Refuse to wear anything too tight, too low, too clingy or to sheer.
- Do not be careless about details such as lose buttons and snaps or hanging hems.
- Never go without hosiery when dealing with the public and be careful or runs in nylons. Remember people see you from the back as well as the front so check heels and tips of shoes and holes in the back of hairdos.
- Run down heels and scuffed dirty shoes are not the look of success.
- Do not wear excessive or cheap perfume. None may be better than too much especially if you work in close quarters with others.

- When you dress, dress in a manner that if you worked for that firm, you would be an asset. For example if you are applying to be a secretary at a law firm, then dress becoming to a law firm in an attractive suit or dress with jacket.
- Never wear slacks for an interview even if you know you can wear slacks on the job.
- If you are applying for a secretarial or a clerical job and you know that the interviewer will be a man, then wear a suit.
- It is best for women who are applying for a professional job to wear a skirted suit. There are always exceptions but generally speaking a suit give off an air of authority and knowledge.
- Blue suits and beige suits are good colors to wear.
- Organization will help you to not have a harried appearance for the interview so get all of your clothes ready the day before so you are not sewing a button on at the last minute.
- Do not wear too many accessories.
- Do not wear too heavy a perfume.
- Dress for the position you want to attain someday.
- When you feel you look good then you can put forth your best foot and have more confidence, so ask yourself before you go out, how confident you feel and if what you are wearing will give the right message to the interviewer.
- You would dress differently if you were up for a job in the fashion industry than you would for a job in a law firm or bank. You can wear more of a fashionable look for a fashion job.
- There are certain general principles to decide what to wear for an interview no matter what kind of company you are anticipating working in.
- The first rule is that whatever you wear should be very comfortable to you both physically and emotionally because nothing is worse than to constantly be tucking a blouse in or wearing a skirt so short you have to keep pulling it down or a wrap skirt that won't stay closed.
- Whatever you are going to wear to the interview it is best to test it and wear it before the interview so that anything that may be a hindrance to comfort can be detected.
- Do not wear a bulky sweater under a suit or a blouse that has too full a sleeve.
- Do not try to create a whole new image for your interview because you probably will end up feeling self conscious.
- Finish off the look with the addition of a simple necklace, belt, or just the right jacket.
- Blouses with soft bows at the neck are very good as well as a string of pearls.
- Posture is an important consideration in an interview, sit tall and stand tall to give an error (aura) confidence. You also look better in your clothes when you have the correct posture.
- Be sure that your grooming is tops because no matter what you wear if your hair is dirty and your shoes are run down, the look you wish to create is destroyed.
- The one situation which it is not smart to venture beyond wearing a jacket is when you have a job interview because it is the safest look when you want to make a good first impression. The jacket conveys at least two different things with the shoulder line

strength and your awareness of professionalism no matter what job you are applying for.

- The jacket does not have to put a huge dent in your budget because there are some wonderful new softer jackets, collarless cardigan type jackets or even the belted jacket which are all good options for women who like jackets but like a change of look.
- The more important the job the more conservatively groomed one should be.
- Do not ever chew gum during an interview.
- A soft daytime make up will enhance ones features but it is more important to just be neat. A healthy glowing skin is a big asset since it says a lot about how the person takes care of herself or himself..
- Loud or weird fantasy eye colors are not good worn during the business day.
- Other things that will be noticed are bad skin and teeth, chewed fingernails and ragged cuticles. These are all indications of how the person takes care of themselves.
- Another noticeable detail that is important are shoes that are not shined and run down heels.
- Conservative styles and colors are best worn to an interview. This means a bright orange jacket with a flowered green and orange blouse might not be best.
- If you want the job and of course you do, then never go to an interview in slacks even if you can wear them on the job.
- Outward appearances are important in an interview but so is how we feel about ourselves on the inside.
- When you walk into a room you immediately give off some kind of impression and it says what kind of image you have of yourself. For instance if you complain about the day or say how stupid you are, you place a negative thought about yourself in the minds of others.
- Put forth an aura of intelligence, sensitiveness, and caring and you will give off positive vibes to the interviewer.
- The sound of your voice is important as well as how you use the English language. If you say we was or they is etc., it will say something about you that will not bring a positive response.
- Organize your thoughts when you are speaking and do not ramble on.
- Use correct posture or body language by sitting and walking tall. The way that you feel about yourself is shown in your body language. The experts say that 60-80% of our communication is done non verbally. This is shown in the way we sit, walk, and enter a room.
- The favorable or unfavorable first impression happens very quickly and if you act like a loser, people will think that way about you.
- If you want to be the winner in a job interview, remind yourself that the person who is the interviewer has shortcomings, inadequacies, and fears also. This makes them more human.
- Be positive and kind.
- Enthusiasm is one of the most important qualities in a personality and is contagious.

- Think of yourself in a very positive way, that you have worth which you do and that you will be an asset to this world. Believe it.
- Because people do form an impression very quickly, it is important that you give a positive impression of yourself. Your facial expressions as well as your words will have a lasting effect and will be evaluated on whether you will be accepted.
- Do not move your head continuously or wring your hands in an interview. Do your best to appear calm and collected.
- You do not have to feel extremely self assured to inspire confidence and be in control. You just need the ability to project that image even if you do not feel it.
- Projecting a negative attitude can keep your ideas from being accepted.
- Being interviewed is a skill that you can and should master because interviews are a part of life.
- Always set up an appointment yourself. It does not make a good impression to have someone else doing your work for you.
- Be sure that you write the appointment time down so that you do not have to call to ask the time again.
- Always be on time.
- Find out if there is anything special they want you to bring for the interview.
- Allow plenty of time for traffic jams, flat tires or any kind of crisis that would put you in a frenzy for the interview.
- Always plan what you will wear ahead of time and dress to look the way you want to be perceived by others.
- If you want to be thought of someone who will fit into a business office, then dress in a more businesslike manner with a suit or dress and jacket.
- If you want a job at a clothing store that is fashionable then wear something that shows off that you have good taste and a fashion flair.
- Think about the job you want and then select an outfit that will help you make a good impression.
- It is a good idea to come to the interview with some knowledge of the office or store and ask intelligent questions.
- One young student that was interviewing with my husband at the University ask," Is this a good school?" His first thought was if you don't know, why bother to apply.
- Posture plays an important part in projecting a positive image. When sitting try to appear relaxed so do not cross your legs and bounce your foot.
- They say interviewers form an opinion about the candidate they are seeing in the first 10-30 seconds.
- If you want to sell yourself to someone else you have to know and like who you are. Go over all of your assets before the interview and see yourself as someone special.
- When shaking hands strive for a handshake that falls somewhere between a steel vise and a damp dishrag.
- Be sure that you make good eye contact. Do not stare but being able to talk eye to eye gives off confidence. Looking down, away or up is distracting and makes you seem insincere or self conscious.

- Think before you speak to cut down on the ums and you knows. It might be a good idea to rehearse with a friend who can see how you sound and where you can improve.
- A tape recorder would be a good idea for picking up those little habits that we don't even realize we have in our speech. Place it in the kitchen or someplace where you are just having a normal conversation and it is easy to pick up some annoying speech habits.
- When an interviewer goes over your application form, you may need to qualify certain facts so be sure you know what you wrote on the form and why you wrote what you did.
- Try not to act shy because you need to be able to talk with enthusiasm and confidence about the things that make you right for the job or school.
- Your ability to get along with others is a key to getting and keeping jobs. No one wants to work with someone who is always complaining or creating problems. Attitude can make or break you.
- It is true that there are many people that apply for a job but it is the little often unnoticed personal habits and grooming details that interviewers look for when they make their final employment decisions.
- If you are too passive you may give off the impression that you are uninteresting and that may be a deciding factor to the interviewer.
- It is always nice to send a note to the interviewer a few days after the interview to thank him or her. It is not always necessary but it can't hurt.
- When leaving an interview always establish eye contact again and leave with a positive thank you and smile.
- It is safest to wear a suit or conservative dress for a job interview.
- Do not dress mannish if you are a woman when interviewing for a job.
- A suit can make the wrong impression for some social service jobs. It may make you seem like you are above rolling up your sleeves and working with people.
- The statistics show that for corporate interviews or jobs in law or finance, the solid color matched suits were the very best. The people in this industry said that they liked the straightforward and self assured look.
- In the less conservative or smaller firms, many women are more comfortable wearing the unmatched suit. The jacket however conveys professionalism but there is room for more femininity and individuality.
- For some of the more creative jobs, a pretty skirt and silk blouse with a shawl or a pretty dress with a vest was positively received.
- Wear clothes that show you respect the firm and are serious about working for them.
- It would be an investment to purchase at least one good outfit, including the shoes, hosiery and pearls if you are not sure of the accessories that will look best.

CHAPTER 8

Ecclesiastes 8:1
"Wisdom brightens a man' s face and changes it' s hard appearance." NIV

PUT ON YOUR BEST FACE — MAKE UP AND SKIN CARE

GENERAL SKIN CARE

- Remove make up thoroughly. Neglect in this area is one of the major causes of skin problems. Use as much time taking makeup off as you do putting it on.
- If you leave dirt behind on your face, it causes a dull looking skin which can make you look older.
- Cleanse and rinse thoroughly, paying particular attention to the areas around the nose, mouth and eye makeup.
- When the body does not have enough water, it will take it from the skin and dry skin will result. They say our outer sin is about 10% water and the deeper layers about 60%. To prevent this from happening, drink at least 6-8 glasses of water a day. Juice or other drinks not included. This is good for the whole body because it will cleanse your system and remove toxins.
- You can help circulation with surface masks and granular scrubs.
- For a lasting glow, try exercise. It promotes good circulation which increases the flow of nourishing blood and oxygen to your skin.

- It is important to maintain the PH of the skin balance. Soaps that have a high ph upset the natural chemical balance and strip the skin of its normal protection and also dry the skin. Soaps like this should be avoided.
- Skin renews itself every 28 days so begin a healthy program today and in about a month there should be marked improvement.
- Always rub your face gently when applying or removing makeup or removing a mask. If you rub harshly or pull downward it can be damaging to your skin.
- So much money is wasted on the wrong colors and kinds of make up so get to know yourself and gain some knowledge into what goes into a good skin care program before putting too much money into your purchase. Knowledge is money.
- Choose a water based moisturizer regardless of skin type. If you do a lot of crash dieting, it will show up on the skin.
- Give up smoking not only for healths sake but for your skin's sake. People who smoke will have more of a tendency to wrinkle.
- Smog is another principle cause of early wrinkles and lifeless skin.
- Start your skin care program when you are young.
- The eye needs special attention because the skin is very delicate and can pulled too tightly when cleaning. This may have a tendency to cause the skin to sag after cleansing this way too long.
- When removing makeup, use a soft cloth or cotton balls. Never use tissues because the paper fibers are rough on the skin.
- Improper food, drinking, smoking, and late hours will show up in figures and faces much earlier than they should.
- It is easier to set up a beautification program than you think. Once you know what you need to do, get it set up, then it becomes automatic like brushing your teeth so get started on a beauty regime that fits you and your life style.
- They are oil based sometimes they can enlarge the pores.
- A wrinkle stick put around the eyes and mouth 2 or 3 times a day helps refresh the moisturizer.
- Get in the habit of using a good cleansing mask.
- Do not wash your face with hot water and harsh drying soaps.
- Stay away from astringents with a lot of alcohol.
- Rough rubbing or strong products used on the skin can make fine lines and wrinkles more noticeable.
- Creams that have cleansing grains in them which take away the top layer of dead skin cells can help your complexion look fresher and brighter.
- A sponge with an abrasive material on it for removing the dead cells should be used with a soft touch.
- Exercise gives circulation a big boost and helps fight stress which relaxes all body muscles including those of the face. Whatever benefits the body will benefit the skin.
- Heredity may offer an advantage but it is up to you to do the rest.
- If you have already gotten an overdose of sun which is one of the worst enemies to the skin, it is not too late to use a sunscreen every day and in every season so you can

stop damage in it tracks and even help the skin to heal itself. However, they say once a wrinkle always a wrinkle.

- Alcohol and cigarettes are very bad for the skin because alcohol dilates the blood vessels and leads to blotching. The theory that smoking is linked with premature wrinkles because it is known to deplete vitamin c which is essential to forming skin supporting collagen. Also creases around the eyes and mouth may be accentuated by puffing and squinting through a haze of smoke.
- A wholesome eating plan that makes you healthy is essential for the best complexion.
- One of the worst things that you can do to your skin is to yo yo diet. The continual losing and gaining of weight can stretch the skin, accentuate wrinkles, break down the supporting skin fibers, and make you look older.
- When the outer layer of skin contains adequate water, it plumps up and looks smoother.
- A good moisturizer will help trap water in the skin.
- To help moisturizer work more effectively, try applying it when your face if a little damp after cleansing.
- Keep an adequate amount of water in your body by drinking 6-8 glasses of water daily.
- Do not push, pull, pinch and squeeze your face as you do your daily cleansing and make up routine. Be gentle so that you do not pull the skin and you will end up with a younger looking skin.
- A clean face is imperative to a healthy looking skin. Light circular motions are best when cleansing the skin.
- Be sure that your hair is pulled back when you cleanse so that you can effectively remove oil in the jawline and hairline.
- It is best to blot the face dry and not pull on it with a towel.
- Check and see that there are no traces of soap or makeup left when you are finished.
- Skin care should not be something that you do one day and then skip a few days. For maximum benefit, it needs to be don consistently. If you do not have a good skin care program or products, consult a good cosmetologist and invest some money in something that will help you the rest of your life.
- The general health of the body is reflected in the skin. Stress causes the glands to secrete oil rapidly and in spurts and then blemishes which are caused by stress begin to pop up.
- Other ways to take good care of your skin is to avoid too much salt, sugar, caffeine, and foods with large amounts of iodine, such as cabbage, shellfish, spinach, and peanuts.
- Try to develop a fixed beauty care routine that you do every day and let it become a habit.
- The eye are does not contain oil glands and is very prone to wrinkling, dark circles, lines, redness and puffiness or a combination of two or more of these problems.
- When removing makeup, use a soft cloth or cotton balls but never use tissues. Paper fibers can be rough on the delicate skin tissues.

- One good way to avoid facial wrinkles is to sleep on your back. If you must use a pillow it is best to use it under the back of the neck so that it doesn't push lines into the face.
- A hit and miss beauty program will not work so keep consistency one of your goals and it will bring you rewards
- Yogurt is good for a sallow skinned person.

MAKE UP

- Evaluate your make up routine to be sure you are not leaving out some important steps.
- Blending is the key to keep makeup soft and use a sponge for blending.
- One of the secrets to putting on makeup and having it look natural and well blended is to use brushes.
- It is as important to look attractive and wear attractive attire around the house for your spouse as much as when you go out. It contributes to good morale when you look your best and make your spouse feel he is important enough to put your make up on.
- Mascara can be a little tricky because some formulas tend to clump on lashes or stick the lashes together. Choose a mascara that goes on smoothly without clumping on the lashes.
- Clean up your makeup tools when done using them to prevent harmful bacteria to your eyes and skin. Use warm sudsy water to clean up and it will be well worth it in the end.
- Check out your makeup techniques by going to a window with natural light and looking at the total effect. Take a soft sponge and blend any hard lines.
- In the morning, if you will apply your foundation and eyeshadow before getting into the bath or shower the moisture helps to set these bases and keep makeup looking fresher longer.
- Make up should not be a cover up but should be a device to bring out your natural beauty. Makeup is like a wardrobe for your face as clothing is for your body.
- Wear make up a little lighter in the day time and add a bit more at night.
- Without a good skin care program, your make up will not be as effective.
- Make up is optional but skin care is a must for every woman.

CIRCLES UNDER THE EYES

- Try to get an adequate amount of sleep
- Too much sleep can sometimes cause circles under the eyes.
- Use a good highlighter cream — one that is lighter than your foundation and lighter than your complexion.
- There are some good stick concealers that could be used also before applying the foundation.
- Blend outward and upward.
- Apply foundation over the highlighter under the eye.
- Keep and light touch — not too heavy a look.

PUFFINESS UNDER THE EYES.

- Do not put highlighter directly to the puffy area because it will tend to make the area more prominent with the lighter shade.
- Darker shades make an area recede so it would be best then to apply concealer in the shadow under and around the puff.
- Moles, birthmarks, pimples and other blemishes can usually be effectively covered up with the same basic highlighting concealing technique that is used to cover up under eye circles and dark spots.
- One of the biggest mistakes that is made in applying makeup is not blending it into the skin. The result is a hard line around the chin and hair area and gobs of color that looks like it does not belong on the face.
- Always take time to smudge your eyeliner with your finger, edge of the applicator, or a Q tip so that you do not have a harsh black or blue line on your eye.
- Make up under eyeglasses looks good and you may have to add a bit more — however, if the lenses are magnified then the makeup will look a little exaggerated under the eye glasses and may be too harsh. Experiment and check with the look in the natural light.
- Be aware that your eyebrows frame your eyes so tweeze them carefully. They should not dominate your face nor be totally invisible.
- Many times when you overtweeze, they may never grow back. To keep the shape of your eyebrows natural, tweeze only underneath and make a neater look in the middle between the brows.
- When tweezing, pull in the direction that the hair grows.
- If you will put a hot towel on your eyebrows and some cream both before and after the tweezing, it will not hurt as much.
- If you have a lot of tweezing to do, go to a reputable cosmetologist and have them professionally waxed.
- If you are going to tweeze your eye brows, put a warm wash cloth on the area to be tweezed first.
- Always remove your makeup before you go to bed. If you do not do this, your skin will pay for it later.
- If you use bright blue or green eyeshadows and they are not completely blended, they will completely mask the color of your eyes. Blues and greens are very hard to blend and look natural as an eye shadow should. You should not look at someone and see two green or blue eyelids going up and down. If you do use them try combining them with charcoal grays or browns which will at least tone them down and help neutralize them.
- The mauve and taupes for the cool skinned people and the earth tones for the warm skinned people have proven to be nice shadows to use.
- Apply foundation to lids first for easier shadow application. To prevent eye make up from running or creasing, dust powder on lids and brow before applying shadow and use the powder shadow.

- For a smoother application of any makeup remember cream goes on cream, powder goes on powder.
- When applying make up be sure that it is put on a clean face.
- Do not let your make up get too old because it can harbor bacteria. It would be best to replace your mascara after 3-4 months.
- Clean all of your sponges and brushes thoroughly with warm soap and water to cut down bacterial count.
- Be careful of the cosmetics at department stores that are being used as testers. They can spread some infections to the mouth if you are not careful.

Becoming more attractive is like almost anything else in that it requires a step-by-step process so don't be bound by what you have decided are your limitations.

FOCUS ON YOUR GOOD POINTS.

Study women who you think are attractive and figure out what it is that pleases your eye. Is it the way that they wear their makeup or their hair style or maybe something elusive like the way that they speak and gesture.

Sometimes people do not see themselves as they are and therefore cannot make the right changes or even discern good advice when they hear it.

Do not get obsessed with your faults and do not blow your faults out of proportion but concentrate on your liabilities and capitalize on them.

Many women who have been known as beautiful women did not have perfect features but their beauty reputation was earned for their warmth, sympathy, and interest in others. Beauty should not be an overconsuming thing but should be a means to an end.

Do not carry a preconceived notice from childhood into adult hood by feeling awkward and unattractive as you were as a child.

To see yourself more realistically, use a mirror and be very honest on changes that need to be made.

Some of the top models are not that beautiful. They work at analyzing themselves and learn to emphasize their best assets and deemphasize their less than perfect parts.

LIPSTICK

- To choose the right lipstick, take a good look at your lips.
- Too thin a lip:
- Try a light lipstick and then apply a gloss over the center of your mouth to highlight the fullest area.
- Too Full a lip:
- Wear darker shades of a low luster lipstick and apply more lipstick on the bottom lip. Try to avoid calling too much attention to your mouth with the bright lip colors.
- Uneven lips

- Try to equalize them by using a dark lipstick your lower lip and then the next lighter shade available on your upper lip. Once again lip liner helps here also.
- To find lip colors that work together, check the numbers on the lipsticks or color charts. The two shades of lipstick should be close in color value, so no one will notice an obvious difference between your upper and lower lips.
- To extend a lip that seem to be a bit droopy, outline the lower lip slightly upward.
- If you know your color key and continue to coordinate what is best for you in color you will not need so many cosmetics because the cool shades will go with everything that you wear and the warm shades with the warm color clothes.
- No make up will look good if you do not have a healthy glowing skin so begin with the basics such as proper nutrition, plenty of exercise, adequate rest, and a correct cleansing program.
- Lipstick is a protector and even if you do not wear a color, you should wear a clear lipstick to protect your lips from sun, wind, and cold.
- Creamy lipsticks have a higher oil content, give a glossier look to lips, and are a softer lipstick than the no smear types.
- Not all lipstick colors go on the same on all women.
- Your best lip colors are the ones that suit your colors season.
- Warm springs or autumns — Peach, tawny, coral, rust, and orange reds.
- Cool-Summers ar winters — Rosy pinks, plumbs, mauves, and blue reds.
- If you have a small mouth, use lighter, glossier shade of lipstick to enlarge.
- If you have a full mouth, use the deeper shades of lip color to make the lip appear smaller.
- If you have a large mouth or lips do not wear the frosty lipsticks to accentuate the mouth.
- Powder your mouth lightly with translucent powder if you have a problem with your lipstick developing fuzzy edges or not lasting.
- The younger women and young girls look best in the glossy lipsticks.
- The best look in applying lipstick is to use a lip liner brush first, then fill in with a lipstick brush.
- Use a lip liner to improve and irregular lip shape.
- Be sure you use the brush to apply over the lip line so there is no definition.
- Lip glosses or gels are best applied with the finger tips.
- If you want the gloss to last longer then use a cream lipstick as a basecoat.
- The experts say that the dyes in lipstick is not absorbed by the lips because the skin on the lips is similar to that on the palms of our hands and soles of our feet and have very few pores.
- One problem is that lipstick will change color on the lip. If it does this, perhaps your body chemistry is causing the problem — however, put a primer coat of foundation on your lips before applying lip color.
- If you do not use lipstick, at least use a smooth coat of lip balm to seal in moisture. It will help lipstick go on smoothly.

- If you use a lip liner, it will help the lipstick from running out of the line onto the creases in the upper lip. Be careful that this liner is blended into the lipstick so that no line shows.
- Generally speaking do not try to extend lipstick out of the natural lipline, blot with tissue and seal with powder for staying power. Some of the experts in cosmetics do extend a thin lip line to make it look fuller but if you attempt to do this, be sure it is done properly.

BLUSH

To keep powder blush from streaking over moisturizer, use the dry on dry principle. When apply blush apply moist blush to foundation then put on a translucent powder and reapply powder blush over the powder.

Blush is one of the most important things that a woman can apply to her face to give her that healthy glow or it can be the most obvious mistake with two little round apple cheeks.

Here are a few blush tips.

- The blush color and lip color should be in the same color family.
- You cannot go by the looks of darkness or lightness of the color by the name given to it. Try it on before you decide.
- Sometime a blush color that looks too deep will blend out to a healthy glow on your skin.
- If you choose a blush shade that is too light it will just sit on your cheek looking artificial.
- Darker skins need a rich brighter blush color.
- Always apply cream blush to cream foundation.
- Do not try to put a powder blush directly onto your foundation for it will blotch. Remember in applying blush, cream goes on cream, powder on powder. Once you have put on a loose translucent powder then you can use the powder blush.
- Powder blush produces a soft matte finish and is easy to brush on when your makeup needs a touch up during the day.
- A cream blush blends well on a foundation makeup and you can use a combination of cream and powder blush if you use a translucent powder.
- Do not bring the color up or close to the eyes and do not bring the color in too close to the nose. If you do this, it will make the eyes look smaller and closes up the face. A good guide is to place your index finger alongside your nose and bring your cheek color no closer to your nose than the outer edge of your finger.
- Do not bring the blush down to far on your face for this will make you look drawn. Stop at a point even with the bottom of your nose or slightly above.
- To blend cream blush, always tap with fingertips or a damp make up sponge. Be sure it is well blended on the edges. Do not rub or pull at your skin.
- Put your blush on softly and place from the outside corner of your temple and stroke on the blush in a wedge on the cheekbone. Do not get too far down on the face.
- When applying blush stroke upward.

- Be careful that the blush color you choose is in harmony with your skin tone. If you are in the cool season you will look better with the rose and blue undertones. The warm season will look better with peachy tones.
- If the blush just sits on your cheek with out easy blending perhaps it is the wrong color for your skin or it is too intense or too soft.

MAKE UP FOR WARM SUMMER MONTHS AND SKIN CARE IN THE SUN

- Warm summer months require different beauty priorities.
- Heat will be the biggest problem to cope with instead of dryness and cold. Hot sun is very drying to skin and hair. so moisturize frequently.
- Increase your intake of water.
- Powder can be a useful make up tool during the hot summer months. Baby powder sprinkled on the body can help to keep you nice and cool.
- Translucent powders for the face are a big help to take the shininess away and also add more of a matte finish.
- If you get a tan, The foundation you usually use may not be as good. Check the change of color so that it still continues to blend well.
- For an extra glow with your make up, brush your blush on the cheeks and give an extra fluff on the forehead, near the hairline, and on the tip of the chin.
- Some eye shadows can be a little brighter when you have a tan.
- Powder makeup is good all summer because it will absorb oil better and lessen the chances of creasing or rubbing and perspiring off.
- Powder type brush will stay on better in hot weather. Use over your translucent powder.
- There are powder type eye pencils for those who wish to wish to experiment with the new summer looks.
- Hot weather can sometimes lead to puffiness around the eyes. Try a couple of slices of cool cucumber on the eyes for a soothing effect. You can feel it work. Slices of raw potato can also help to reduce puffiness.
- Moisturizers are important during the spring and summer but for different reasons than used in the winter.
- You secrete more oil from the heat in the summer after being in the sun, so you may not need as much moisturizer. However, protect your skin from losing water at night with a good moisturizing cream.
- Don't forget to give your neck the same care as that you give your face.
- Daylight in summer is especially intense so be sure to avoid shiny and frosted lipsticks which will look artificial in bright light. It is better to use one that leaves a more natural looking finish.
- The no smear lipsticks give more lasting protection than the softer lipsticks that come off on the food you eat.
- Choose a lipstick that will stay on when swimming and this will help keep your lips from getting irritated from the sun, perspiration, and water.

- Lips tend to get dry and chapped during the summer and lipstick will help seal and protect them.
- If the sun has dried your lips out and caused some tiny creases around your mouth, avoid the greasy lipsticks because they will have more of a tendency to spread into these furrows.
- Use some softer shades such as coral for the warm skinned people and the soft rose and pinks for the cool skinned woman.
- In the summer time when everyone dons a pair of sunglasses, be a little careful not to get the frames out of proportion to your face size 7.
- When applying eye make up, if you have protruding or puffy eyes, use the darker shades and avoid light or frosted colors.
- To some degree your health is reflected in your lips. If they are healthy they will probably be moist and rosy However if they are pale or dull you may need to be aware of increasing your nutrition. For instance eating yogurt, apricots, Taking Vit. B complex or brewers yeast may put a little more color into them.
- For dry lips, try to increase your intake of foods with polyunsaturated vegetable oils and increase your protein.
- If your lips are very dry, do not go outdoor with them unprotected. Wear lipstick, gloss, or a chapstick.
- When you wear lipstick, it lessens the chance of chapping because it is a protector and seals in the natural moisture. When this natural moisture evaporates from sun, wind, heat, or dry climate, your lips can become sensitive, irritated, cracked and even bleed so keep them adequately protected.

TANNING

You have heard it said over and over that sun is your worst enemy on aging skin. Blue eyed blonds and redheads usually burn and freckle while the olive toned skin usually takes on a smooth rich color. But whoever you are, the effects of too much sun will be a thickened and weathered skin texture with premature wrinkles.

- The higher the number on the sun block lotion, the more protection you get.
- If you have burned once, it will make you more susceptible to another bad burn.
- Many people lie in the sun to help clear up acne, however, a little sun goes a long way in drying out the skin. There is a mistaken notice that if they get burned and peel, the acne will disappear but acne is systemic and overexposure to the sun is not the answer.
- If you get swollen sunburned lips, then use special care around the mouth. There are special sunstick lip protectants on the market as well as lip balms.
- One expert I asked said that zinc oxide put on the lips is a good protector. It doesn't look pretty however and be sure you are not allergic to zinc.
- If suntan lotions do not work for you, perhaps you are not using it properly. It has to be applied and reapplied while exposed to the sun. One time usually doesn't do it. Perspiration, and going in the water all remove some protection.

- If you have been burned bad enough to blister or if your skin becomes swollen, then see a doctor.
- Do not try to acquire a tan in a day or a weekend. Take the sun in small doses.
- When you are near water the extra refection of the sun requires extra protection. This is true of overcast days as well.
- Take a good sunblock with a SPF of at least 15.
- Apply the sun block whenever sunbathing or around the water.
- Apply before and after swimming.
- Take a hat for added protection to the face.
- Sun tan slowly by starting with 15 to 20 minute exposures and work up gradually from there. Do not wait until you see red before you cover up.
- In the summer, switch to a light water based foundation to avoid the shiny look on your face.
- Eyeshadows are good protection against burned eyelids. Powder shadows are best in summer and do not get soft on your lids and run.
- Lipstick is an important addition because the intense sun will tend to dry your lips and cause them to chap and peel.
- Lips do not have oil producing glands so you should always make a conscious effort to protect them.
- Remember to moisturize not only on the outside but from the inside also in the hot weather. Drink plenty of fluids to replenish what is lost through perspiration.
- Also eat fruits and vegetables daily because they are very good for the skin.
- To reduce peeling, moisturize all over with a rich lotion.
- Do not over look moisturizing the back of the knees, tops of feet, elbows, ears and your neck.
- Sun affects the different skin types in different ways. For instance, blonds and red-heads are the most likely to be sun sensitive and burn faster than those with darker complexions. A darker skin has a protective pigment that works like a shield against the sun.
- Be smart when you tan and tan gradually
- Sun condition your skin by limiting the amount of time you spend in the sun according to your skin tone. Start with 10 min. a day and increase 5 min. a day.
- Use a good sunscreen to block the burning rays and let the tanning rays through.
- Sun protection factor lotions which are between 2 and 15 indicate how much protection you will get from the sunscreen. The higher the number, the more protection.
- For instance, if you could stay in the sun for 15 minutes without burning, then with a sunscreen that has a sun protection factor of 2 would allow you would be able to stay out twice as long or 30 minutes without burning
- Apply sunscreen evenly, and always reapply right after swimming.
- Pay special attention to hot spots like the nose, cheeks, knees and lips because they can be forgotten in the sun and get a real burn.
- The sun is the most intense between 11 a.m.. and 3 p.m.. so be very careful.

- Do not forget that you can burn while swimming because the sun rays go right through the water so count the time swimming as time sunning.
- At the beach, the sun can bounce off the sand and right under an umbrella or hat.
- Snow is one of the worst culprits bouncing back up to 85% of the burning rays.
- Don't be fooled by haze and fog because it will allow ultraviolet light through and give a real rememberable burn.
- Take some breaks in your day to save you from too much tension that is bound to show up in your skin.
- Neglect of a good skin care program shows up first on our neck and the hands. Even before time begins to reveal itself here, moisturize consistently.
- Take the sting out of a sunburn by soaking in a tub filled with lukewarm water and three or four tea bags. The tannic acid can be very soothing.

COLD WEATHER TIPS

- Cold crisp winter air is invigorating but it is hard on the skin. Strong winds and low humidity deplete the skin of moisture and leave it dry, flaky, or scaly. Sometimes when the office or home is too hot which makes the humidity low , it can have the same effect.
- Do not sit in a very hot tub of water too long and when you do bathe keep the bath and shower water tepid. Hot water dehydrates the skin and breaks down the natural oil barrier. The longer you soak the more water your skin loses.
- Be careful of the kind of soap that you use and chose one suited to your skin type. Do not use soap on your face unless it is a specially made soap for faces.
- If your skin is very dry, use a cream cleanser.
- For the greatest benefit, moisturize your face and body immediately after bathing while you are still damp. The moisture will help trap water in your skin.
- A humidifier at home or in the office can help the dry skin problems. If you do not have one try boiling some water on your stove that will give off some humidity.
- Whenever you go out into wintery weather, cross country skiing, an early morning jog, or even a quick trip to the super market, the winter winds and sudden change in temperature steal essential fluids from your skin.
- Your oil gland output slows down after age 25 and then slows even more before menopause so your skin care regimen should increase with moisturizers.

CHAPTER 9

Luke 12:7
"But even the very hairs of your head are all numbered....." KJV

HELP WITH HAIR

Your hair should be one of the most positive image impressions that you have. Not only is it one of the first things that people notice about you but it also offers you the most immediate area of change to improve your image. The way that you wear your hair, the color you put on it and the kind of condition it is in all reflect a style and indicate a definite statement about yourself. If you will step out on faith and cut and experiment with color and a new style you can create a whole new look and one that will perhaps takes years off your looks. If a persons hair does not look good, it seems like other things just do not matter.

SHAMPOO

- Hair should be squeaky clean at all times.
- Wash your hair as often as you need to and do not worry about washing it too much. A mild shampoo should clean quickly and efficiently.
- Be sure all shampoos are rinsed from the hair thoroughly.
- Choose a shampoo that does not have paraben in it because it can coat the hair and soon it will not curl because of being coated with the shampoo. Many shampoos may coat the hair so ask your hairdresser to recommend a good one. If you buy one in the store, read the label to see if it does have the coating ingredient in it

- Treat your hair gently as possible after washing by squeezing out the excess water and not rubbing vigorously.
- A healthy scalp is very important to a healthy head of hair.
- Do not automatically assume that a scaling scalp means that you have dandruff because it could be caused by several things.
- Too much exposure to sunlight and the scalp has become sunburned.
- Residue left in the hair after shampooing
- The use of hair spray or setting lotion
- Before you switch to a dandruff shampoo, give your regular shampoo a chance to work by rinsing it out more thoroughly.
- Treat dry scalp with a light oil massage.
- Leave hairspray and setting lotions off your hair for a week or two.
- How often you shampoo varies with the type of hair and scalp you have, your hair style and personal preference.
- Do not use a shampoo that will coat your hair such as the ones that claim to thicken the hair. Consult with your beautician because if you get a build up of wax coating on your hair, it will not only not look shiny but it will not curl easily.
- Since your hair takes a lot of abuse from styling, blow drying, and over heated rooms, the use of creme rinses or deep conditioners can improve the feel and texture of the hair.

HAIR STYLE AND FACE SHAPE

- A good competent hairdresser is a must to get a cut that not only can be easily styled but will fit your face shape.
- A round face needs hair to feather forward to the chin. This softness slims the roundness.
- The long angular rectangular face can be shortened if you swirl bangs from the crown and taper hair to the chin. Do not wear hair straight down on the sides.
- The square face needs some feather bangs that wave to the temples and a soft pageboy at the jawline.
- Diamond face shapes need soft bangs to give the illusion of a broader forehead with width at the jawline.
- The pear shaped face needs to add volume and fulness at the temples with a soft fuller more curly style.
- Heart shaped faces should keep hair close to the crown and temple to deemphasize the fullness of the forehead and cheekbones. Add softness and fullness at the chinline.
- The perfect shaped face is the oval and you can wear your hair in almost any style.
- As I mentioned in make up, a good way to fine out your face shape is to stand in front of a mirror with a lipstick or bar of soap and draw the outline of your face onto the mirror. This will give you a pretty good idea where you are wide and narrow.
- Hair and nails can be a real barometer of your health. Sometimes when hair falls out, there is a thyroid deficiency.

- During the warm months, have your hair trimmed more frequently than usual. They say that hair grows faster in the summer and exposure to the elements of summer causes split ends.

HAIR COLOR

- The right hair color can brighten your whole face, flatter your skin tones, light up your eyes and bring out your personality.
- Softer lighter hair colors tend to project an overall friendlier image.
- Too bright a hair color can create a stern look.
- Any color change in your hair whether it is a subtle change or dramatic depends on your own natural hair color plus your skin tone. Here is another good reason to know your color key, cool or warm.
- Start with the color you have. If it is mousey or drab, add a few highlights to give it a sunny look, or maybe even a little lighter.
- A good way to find out what you will look like in a certain color is to try on some wigs.
- Warm hair colors , those with the reddish or golden undertones, seem to bring things closer to you and they seem to stand out to the observer more.
- The ashen hair colors, those with no reddish or golden undertones are receding colors and make things look farther away, smaller or camouflaged.
- If your face is too round, it can be made to look slimmer with a side part and adding color highlights at the top.
- A too thin face can be made to look broader by adding fullness at the sides and a hair color lighter than your own.
- Too sharp a face features can be softened with a curly hair do and a lighter hair color.
- To make deep-set eyes appear larger and wider, pull the hair toward the face at the forehead and add some blond highlights at the temples.
- If your forehead is too high, cover it with bangs and highlight hair from crown to tips of bangs and sides to play up the eyes.
- If you have never colored or lightened your hair, take it easy because too little is better than too much.
- Gray hair can be beautiful and very attractive. However, most of us fight gray hair all of our lives. There is no scientific evidence to say that stress causes gray hair. Gray hair most often occurs as a natural part of the aging process and heredity plays a very important role in determining when and how quickly this process occurs.
- Some of the other causes of gray hair are a metabolic upset, nervous system problem, endocrine gland disorder, physical or mental shock, or severe illness.
- Graying because of age is irreversible, however if the graying results from other causes, color may come back to the hair when the person recovers from the illness.

GENERAL TIPS ON HAIR:

- They say that fish is brain food but it is also hair food. That is because fish are full of minerals and zinc which makes for healthy and shining hair.

- Nutrition of the hair is very important. Since your hair is actually old protein, it cannot receive nourishment from vitamins in any hair care products. There are varied opinions on this because some companies say they can put protein into the hair but unless you have a good balance of protein in your diet, your hair will not have the glow of health.
- Many additives in shampoos and rinses may simply coat your hair strands.
- A good balanced diet including vitamins and minerals will help maintain growth of strong healthy looking hair
- Your hair will survive a certain amount of abuse but if you want beautiful hair, the key word is care.
- Hair is said to grow faster between the ages of 15 and 25.
- Cutting the hair does not affect the hair growth although removing the split ends improves the appearance.
- Hair grows on the average of l/4 to l/2 inch a month.
- Put peanut butter on your fingers and rub it into your hair to remove chewing gum from the hair. The gum should come loose and then wash as usual.
- Beautiful hair is essential to good grooming.
- Do not ever say to others with your appearance in curlers in public that that is how you feel about yourself.
- If your diet does not include a wide variety of nutrients from which your hair can feed, no amount of hair care techniques will help.
- The first way to stop hair abuse is to stop using the wrong products.
- Everyday blow drying or hot roller styling will also abuse your hair and dry it out.
- Be care in the hair ornaments and hair fasteners that you choose because sharp edges on barrettes and uncoated plastic will break you hair in no time at all.
- Make sure that you brush every day to get out every trace of styling material or hair spray.
- It is best not to attempt complicated chemical processing of the hair at home. You may end up spending more in the end to have a professional correct your mistakes rather than having it done right in the first place.
- The only way to get rid of split ends is to cut them off so it is best to take precautions to avoid them before they get started by taking care of your hair.
- Proper reconstructing of the hair by professionals with proper products will help to slow down split ends.
- Products recommended for your specific hair type and problem areas are always the best to use.
- The biggest help in taking care of hair is to get it cut right and shaped correctly for your hair texture and your face shape.
- If you hair loses its shine when you are exercising vigorously, the culprit is probably perspiration so wash out frequently.
- Hair that is all different lengths and going every which way makes grow out time harder than it seems to be. Even if you have to have a little length removed your hair will look better and be easier to manage.

- You could be brushing you hair with the wrong brush. Wide set plastic bristles fluff the hair and they are best used to add lift and volume to any style. Thicker, denser bristles either natural or nylon will smooth hair.
- Get a professional perm which will enable you greater styling freedom with little or no trouble.
- Many women fight with their hair all their lives because they are afraid to get a permanent but a good perm will build body in your hair. Now days they have been improved to give you curls, or just a body wave or even they have spot perms. Have your hair in really good condition first.
- Sometimes before a permanent is given, the hair needs to be stripped to get the build up of hair products off of the hair. Commercial stripping products are best to be used for this problem. Your hairdresser can advise you on this matter.
- After you perm, get frequent trims to snip off any split ends.
- Sometimes the hair will get more manageable with some good gels and lotions. Using too much however, can leave the hair sticky and difficult to manage and style.
- We work at hair level when styling our hair but the hair dresser works from above and hair is a lot easier to guide and manage from that angle so raise your arms above your head and reach down.
- For a quick hair pick up, use some of the fashionable barrettes and combs to get hair out of the way and give it a sleek more pulled together appearance.
- To get volume in your hair, us a soft hair spray and spray the hair thoroughly, brushing the spray through the hair for an even distribution. Allow the spray to dry for a few minutes and bend over and brush hair down for volume, stand up and shake the hair into place, brush lightly again.
- If your hair get wilted in the hot humid weather, try pulling the sides of your hair back with some beautiful combs or change your part to the other side which will give you a fuller look.
- Healthy hair shines because it reflects light and if hair is in good condition light will be reflected but if your hair is damaged, light will be scattered rather than reflected and the overall look will be dull.
- Overprocessing can dull the hair also.
- The overuse of certain hair care products such as conditioners or hairspray can leave a dulling buildup and hair will look drab if it is not rinsed thoroughly after shampooing.
- Over exposure to sunlight which bleaches and dries out hair can be a number one duller so always wear a hat or scarf when you are out in the sun a long time.
- A rich conditioner should be used especially during the hot summer months.
- Do not forget to protect your hair when you are swimming because chlorine attacks the protein in the hair and salt water can be very drying. Tucking your hair under a swimming cap may be a good idea.
- If there is low humidity it will make your hair dull because it saps the moisture from the hair and makes it more dry. Always use a good moisturizer for the hair if you live in a dry climate.

- The use of hard water can dull the hair because its minerals may combine with the shampoo and leave a residue. If you have this problem use a good acidic rinse. You can do this yourself by mixing l/2 cup apple cider vinegar with 4 cups of water.
- Pollution in the air is a big duller of hair and the solution is to shampoo more often.
- If you have been sick or unusually stressed, your sebaceous glands produce more oil so dust and dirt can collect on the hair more readily making it dull and limp. Use a shampoo for oily hair at this time.
- It will only take a matter of weeks for a poor diet to show up in your hair. Protein is a major component of hair.
- Don't forget to cover your head from the sun because the sun's rays will fade your hair color. There are a lot of fashionable hats, turbans, and scarves so choose what suits your personality.

A FEW NATURAL HAIR TIPS

Here are a few natural hair tips for those who do not want to spend a lot of money on the manufactured hair care products.

- Between shampoos, sprinkle corn meal in the hair to loosen dust particles and brush out.
- Use baking soda on the scalp to blot up excess oils, and then brush to remove the granules of powder and then rub down with a dry towel to restore shine.
- To enhance body and luster to hair, mix a raw egg into the normal amount of shampoo needed to suds the hair clean. Lather as usual, but be sure to rinse with cold water.
- Other natural ingredients known to add shine to the hair are white vinegar rinses, lemon juice, or witch hazel. Two of three tablespoons of these should be mixed with at least a quart of warm water and used as a final rinse. Be sure to rinse thoroughly.
- Brewed tea rinses are said to bring out the natural highlights and are easy to make. The teas to use are camomile or marigold buds and work well on hair of all colors. Brews made from shelled walnuts or sliced beets are for brunettes only.
- Excellent hair conditioners are mayonnaise and oils such as olive, sesame, soybean, and safflower. Mayonnaise may be cool or at room temperature but the oil should be warmed before applying. After shampooing and rinsing, towel dry your hair a little to get rid of excess moisture and use enough mayonnaise or oil to completely coat hair, work it in with your fingers, then wrap head in a plastic wrap to retain body heat that helps the oil penetrate. Shampoo and rinse thoroughly.
- Natural products can be beneficial to your hair, but the most important ingredients are physical and emotional health.
- The only way to get rid of split ends is to cut them off.

HAIR LOSS

- If you continue to lose your hair over weeks and months with no apparent regrowth, see your doctor and have some thyroid function tests.

- One of the reasons that women experience hair loss after 40 is in hormones and heredity. Some women and many men are born with genes that lend itself toward baldness.
- Men who lose hair seem to see the front hair line recede until only a horseshoe rim of hair remains over the ears and around the back of the head. A woman however, tends to retain the front hairline and the hair on the crown may get very thin. Hairs that remain on her head are smaller in diameter than they once were and grow at a slower rate, and she will usually not become totally bald as a man does.
- Temporary hair loss may be traced to stress in many cases. Once the stress is relieved, the hormonal balance is restored and normal hair growth can resume.
- Wigs and toupees have been a satisfactory way to replace hair. The new wigs and toupees look very natural and are made with human hair so they can be styled at home. It is not any more trouble than doing ones own hair.
- Many times you do not need a full wig but you can sometimes get a hair piece and pin it to the existing hair and then comb it so there is no line between hair piece and your own hair. It could be matched to the natural color and texture and no one would ever know the difference.
- Losing hair is a very traumatic thing for both men and women. As we age, some decrease in hair count is perfectly normal.
- Each morning check your pillow case for excessive hair loss. Sometimes as imbalance in thyroid can cause hairlessness.
- Sometimes following a fad diet will increase hair loss, especially one that restricts protein.
- Another cause could be a major surgery or a long illness, an infection with a high fever, or a period of prolonged stress. Any of these causes can be temporary.
- Some medications can lead to thinning of the hair also.
- One dermatologist suggested that wheat germ and peanuts may aggravate hair loss.
- Another cause could be tight braid or ponytails.
- Permanent hair loss from follicle destruction can result from prolonged pulling on the hair. It is best not to use tight curlers, clips, hairpins, and stiff hair brushes.
- A soft natural bristle brush is the best one.
- If the hair is thinning, a wide tooth comb with smooth rounded ends would be better than a brush.
- Average amounts of hair processing, coloring, and permanents don't affect hair growth or loss. But women who do these processes too frequently will accelerate the tendency to temporarily thin hair on top.
- Intensive programs of exercise and scalp massage have never been shown to be a help but what has been shown is that too vigorous scalp massage can contribute to hair loss because of hair abuse. The basic rule that doctors do agree on is to be as gentle as possible with your hair.

CHAPTER 10

Proverbs 15:17
"Better a meal of vegetables where there is love than a fattened calf with hatred." NIV

IT MAY NOT BE FUN TO DIET AND EXERCISE, BUT IT'S FUN TO LOOK AND FEEL GOOD

It seems that everyone has been on some kind of a diet sometime in their lives. Every one would like some kind of magic wand to lose weight and inches but the realistic truth is that it take work, self control and self discipline, persistence and consistency. When you think about it if someone did have a magic wand it would not be as rewarding to have set a goal and accomplished it. One of the reasons that people need to diet so much is their diet. With so many fast food places and junk food available, it makes it easy to eat and easy to put on added pounds.

DIET TIPS

- Start a diet with a positive note by going out and buying something for yourself that will look good on you right now. When you are losing pounds and inches, it is important that you look as good as possible in the process.
- It would be advantageous for you to wear your best colors in clothes and in makeup because your most flattering colors are going to make you look the best.

- Keep yourself busy doing things that do not involve food because many times the favorite thing for us to do is centered around food.
- If you do not have enough to do to keep busy, then do some volunteer work or do other things that keep you away from the refrigerator.
- There are many calories consumed in front of the TV so perhaps when you are watching for an evening have some carrot sticks or celery sticks or some non fattening food to munch instead of the potato chips etc.
- Always check with your doctor before beginning an exercise program but exercise and diets go together for the maximum amount of benefit.
- It is important to have someone who will reinforce you and encourage you. It is hard to lose weight all alone. This is why support groups are excellent.
- Find someone who is on a diet also, and share your feelings together. It is important to have people who will cheer you on and keep telling you that you can do it.
- After you lose weight the hardest thing to do is to keep it off because perhaps your metabolism lends itself to weight gain so you will have to make up your mind to change your eating life style forever. If you were used to a snack at bedtime that habit may have to change.
- When you eat sugar, your craving for sugar is increased so the best thing is to not eat sugar at all or at least keep it to a minimum. It is not good for your digestive system anyway.
- If you get used to cutting out sugar, you will get so your body will not handle it well and when you eat something like a candy bar, it will not make you feel well.
- There are substitutes for sugar such as raw honey and if you use this you need to use half a teaspoon of baking soda per cup of honey and one or two tablespoons less liquid in your recipe.
- You can look pounds thinner if you learn to dress with the correct line, style and color. See figure problems.
- There are a lot of fad diets around with different ideas on losing weight but the best way to diet is under supervision with nourishing meals.
- Keep your refrigerator stocked with good snacks like fresh yogurt, fresh fruits and vegetables so that if the hunger pangs come you will have something that is low in fat and nourishing to eat.
- There are some days when dieting is impossible such as family get togethers, holidays and vacations. Learn to cut back before and after the event and enjoy yourself.
- Eat sunflower and sesame seeds to improve your memory and powers of concentration.
- If you want to be fit and healthy, it is better to be slim. Overweight predisposes you to many chronic ailments and you have more chance of dying of stroke and coronary heart disease.
- Diets have a high failure rate. Before you can break the vicious cycle of dieting and successfully manage to lose weight you must examine your attitudes towards yourself, the food that you eat or do not eat, and the various pressures exerted upon you by society.

- It has been shown that people under stress eat more often.
- Not every one responds to pressure by eating. To establish how stress sensitive your appetite is, look back over your recent stresses. If you put weight on immediately afterwards, then perhaps one of the keys to your weight problem in the future is to simply be aware of how you react under stress and seek a different outlet.
- Destructive eating habits take some time to break so do not be discouraged by set-backs.
- Suck a slice of lemon or dill pickle. The sourness will affect your tastebuds and may eliminate your craving for sweets.

SOME REASONS FOR NOT BEING ABLE TO LOSE WEIGHT ON A DIET AND MORE DIET TIPS

- You may need more activity to burn up more calories, so how is your exercise program?.
- Don't try to diet without exercise to firm you up.
- Another reason may be that the metabolic and chemical changes taking place in the body maybe quite drastic when you start to diet. You may go for weeks on a diet and not experience weight loss while your body is going through this change.
- Reduce your plate size as well as the amount of food on the plate.
- Be care of a negative attitude developing about the diet and how it is restricting you. Feeling sorry for yourself because you are on a diet may cause you to become must less active and enthusiastic, thus not burning up enough calories.
- Do not start your diet on the week end. It is best to start in Monday and then by the weekend you will adapt better to it and will not be so tempted to go off the diet.
- Weigh yourself once a week. Any more often than that may be self defeating. The A. M. is the best time to weigh.
- If you will keep busy, then you will not think of food as often.
- Never eat when you are emotionally upset.
- Be sure that you eat balanced nutrition from the four food groups.
- Boost your energy level with a quick nourishing snack such as cheese or an apple.
- If you are counting calories, instead of a calorie laden soft drink, try iced mineral water with a slice of lime or lemon.
- Add grapefruit to your diet because it simulates faster digestion and fat deposit breakdown.
- Cut out sweets.
- If you will eat slowly and chew your food well, you will find that you will eat less.
- Start your meal with soup and salad and it will cut down on the regular food that you eat.
- Eat smaller portions of food at more frequent intervals throughout the day.
- There are many theories on how to diet and what to eat but until we in our own minds want to reach a weight goal we will not be too successful.
- Keep healthy snack foods such as fruits and vegetables more handy than sweets.
- Prepare your mind before you start a diet.

- Avoid the long term diets especially the ones that advocate a bizarre or highly restricted range of food.
- Balance is more important not less important when you are slimming and eating considerable less than you normally would.
- It is unwise to just cut out meals not only because of the nutritional aspect but I heard a doctor say that when people go on diets and cut out meals, their metabolism slows down and consequently does not burn up the fat. When one is eating three planned meals a day, that keeps the metabolism fat burning process going.
- It is important to drink plenty of water preferably eight to ten glasses a day and avoid diets that suggest you should restrict your fluid intake. The body loses about 3-31/2 pints of water a day and it is essential that this fluid is replaced.
- The less you eat the more fluid you should drink.
- Be a bit skeptical when reading the latest diet fad or wonder food.
- Avoid slimming aids that may affect the normal function and metabolism of your body unless prescribed by your doctor.
- Be aware that many of the slimming pills have side effects such as agitation, irritability, sleeplessness and a raised heart beat. Also, many depress you while they are depressing your appetite.
- Over eating is by the greatest cause of overweight.
- There are some indications that too frequent and over stringent dieting may affect the bodies capacity to readjust to normal food intake once the diet is over.
- Continual bouts of crash dieting is bad for the figure, bad for your health, and may turn out to be self defeating.
- Suck on an ice cube to satisfy your urge to snack without adding calories.
- The amount of calories you need to maintain your body weight depends on several factors — activity, bone structure, metabolism and climate.
- As we age we need fewer calories because our rate of metabolism declines and we probably will be less active.
- There is some evidence that more calories are expended in colder climates.
- If you want to lose one pound a week you have to cut your present calorie intake by 500 calories a day.
- Diets that focus on one particular food will leave the dieter without energy and will give the dieter dull brittle hair.
- Skipping a meal is not a good idea unless you want to be twice as hungry later.
- Set realistic goals. Aiming for 20 pounds lost in two weeks is not a realistic goal.
- You may be a person that needs someone looking over their shoulder and having to be accountable to them to be able to keep on your weight plan and reach your goal.
- Unless you have all the will power in the world, a diet that is complicated will not be easy to stick to.
- Tomato juice has fewer calories than orange or apple. Tomato is only about 25 calories per half a cup, orange is 55 and apple is 62.

- The morning meal is about the most important of the day. Your body has been without food for many hours and it needs to be refueled — however, coffee and a jelly donut is not what your body needs.
- When you eat sugar for breakfast, it sends your blood sugar rate on a roller coaster ride and when your blood sugar falls, then your energy level falls also. This can leave you feeling irritable, depressed and tired.
- If you continue unhealthy health habits even though you may feel o.k. now, it will eventually catch up with you.
- The traditional breakfast of bacon, egg, and toast is not a necessity. A good breakfast can consist of fruits and vegetables and add a carbohydrate and a protein. Try stepping out of the tradition by eating a piece of toast with peanut butter on it or a tuna fish sandwich.
- Get into the habit of reading labels on the foods that you buy and be aware that the ingredient that is listed first is what it contains the most of. If sugar is listed first on a cereal box, it contains more sugar than the other ingredients. Some of the cereals are 50% sugar.
- Get out of the old breakfast routine and serve soups or even a breakfast salad which can be nutritional and take the boredom out of breakfast as well.
- Try a breakfast shake which takes only a few minutes to prepare in your blender. Combine l cup of milk, l egg, l cup strawberries or l medium banana and one tsp. of vanilla.
- Leftovers make a great breakfast treat such as a slice of left over quiche or cold fruit salad.
- Try a cottage cheese sundae and top it with your favorite fruit and sprinkle with sunflower seeds. Canned fruit is very good on cottage cheese when fresh fruits are not in season.
- Health starts on the inside.
- Keep some wheat germ flakes on hand to sprinkle on your toasts or cereal to add some extra vitamin B to your diet. Wheat germ flakes need to be kept refrigerated.
- To beat the blues when you are dieting, avoid foods made up of refined sugar and flour.
- Keep your vitamin B level up with beef, fish, broccoli, brussel sprouts, chicken and cottage cheese.
- A calcium deficiency can cause low moods so be sure your diet includes sufficient amounts of cheeses, milk products, beans, and broccoli.
- Do not drink cup after cup of black coffee because it has no calories. Coffee can destroy Thiamine or Vit. Bl and in doing this a blue mood can get worse.
- If you are dieting and you crave a drink that is hot, try hot water and a teaspoon of unsweetened lemon juice instead of coffee. It has only three calories. tastes tangy, and works great as a natural diuretic.
- If you begin to look drawn and tired in the middle of a diet, that drawn look will be gone in a month or so after your body fat redistributes.

- Try not to be obsessed by the scale. Weigh yourself once a week because weighing yourself daily only sets you up for some disappointment.
- When purchasing food from the supermarket instead of buying the ones that are labeled light, look for products that are marked low calorie or reduced calorie. Reduced calorie products must have at lease one third fewer calories than other similar foods.
- When you read the ingredient list, sugars and fats should be lower on the label since these are the two substances usually reduced when foods are lightened in calories.
- Look for labels that say low fat.
- Read all of the label when shopping because sometimes the protein and vitamins content is reduced along with the calories.
- If there is a brand name food you use regularly that does not list the nutritional information, then buy a different one that does.
- Many diets end up being deficient in calcium. It is a very important part of our diet and keeps the bones and teeth healthy. Calcium starts leeching out of our bones in our mid twenties and is one of the major aging ailments called osteoporosis. This means you have to build up a healthy reserve. The calcium intake of women averaged 12% below the recommended daily dietary allowance.
- Women are eight times more likely than men to develop osteoporosis. One of the reasons is pregnancy and breast feeding divert calcium from mother to child and another reason is that women are more likely to go on weight reducing diets, many of which are low in calcium. Also, women have less bone mass than men.
- Some major sources of calcium are milk and milk products, cheese, ice cream, and low fat yogurt as well as many vegetables.
- Eating more protein than your body needs accelerates calcium loss.
- Make sure that you get enough vitamin D, either through sunlight or diet because it aids the body's absorption of calcium.
- The body is an organism that continually renews itself so it needs good nutrition to rebuild cells and beauty requires a well balanced diet.
- If you do not change your eating habits, your weight will go right back up when you go off of your diet.
- It is important for you to find a brand new food plan that will fit in with your life style and to know the calories that you need to maintain your ideal weight and feel well.
- Everyone has a different idea of what will work and what will not so you have to find out what is right for you.
- One interesting theory on dieting is that to maintain a healthy weight, most of the eating one does should be done from noon to 8 p.m.. with nothing but fruit from the morning hour to noon and after 8 in the evening.
- Another theory states that it is what is eaten with what that helps to maintain proper body health and weight.
- Try fooling your stomach by eating more slowly. Your food will seem like more and also spread your calories over five small meals rather than three large ones.
- When the portions are small, serve them on smaller plates and take larger portions of low calorie foods like salads.

- The most effective diet is a lifetime habit of intelligent low calorie eating which can become part of our lifestyle in far less time than one would think.
- Don't fool yourself into thinking that once the weight is off you'll simply stay that way. If you fall back into your old eating habits and ways of thinning you will probably end up back at your old weight.
- Know your food weaknesses. We all have them like chocolate, cake, potato chips etc. If you have a hard time giving up these goodies, try freezing a candy bar and when the craving gets too much, cut a small piece off and let it melt in your mouth to take the edge off your craving.
- If you find you cannot eat just a little, then avoid having your danger foods around at all.
- Make a list of tension releasing activities that will relax you instead of eating. Go for a walk, call a
- friend, write letters, read a good book, but break the eating because of stress habit.
- Take charge of your life because its your hand that holds the fork or spoon and gets the extra calories in your mouth or you can choose not to.
- Do not blame other people for your slipups. People may make you nervous but they do not make you eat.
- Lose weight for yourself and for your own self esteem not for someone else.
- If you gain a few pounds back, do not let your weight stray too far before losing again.
- Exercise can cross out those extra calories from eating things that you should not have eaten.
- Exercise helps burn up fat and make muscles lean. Exercise will help you maintain your weight a lot longer.
- Many times we think that if I just lose weight I will be happier but that doesn't always solve our problems. We need to accept ourselves as we are and look at ourselves in a positive way so that not only is our figure in better shape but our self image is improving also. Look inside yourself and figure out what makes you eat more than you need. Losing weight really begins on the inside of our head.
- Make note of your eating habits. When you find yourself eating at certain times other than mealtime, then do something or plan something for that time period so you won't be eating. Many times we eat because we are bored or just out of habit.
- Try some tricks to keep you from eating too much.
- Try keeping track of the calories your have resisted during the day rather than the calories you have eaten.
- Do not eat anything unless you are sitting at the dining room table. This means dinner, or even just a cracker.
- Make a rule for yourself that you cannot eat anything in front of the TV. If you are going to eat something, go to the dining room table and if you do this chances are you will not bother.
- It is always good to have your goals and your progress on paper where you can see it, so make yourself a weight chart on a graph and keep it where you can check your progress.

- Give yourself rewards for reaching weekly goals.
- Put a reward for yourself in the refrigerator nicely wrapped and everytime you open the refrigerator you will see it waiting for you. When you reach that short term goal you can take it out and use it. Then set another short term goal, put another reward in the refrigerator and go for it. One lady said she did this and it worked but she went one step further. She gave herself a time limit and if she did not reach her short term goal by the time allotted, she had to give the reward away.
- Another good tip is to set inch by inch goals. To try and say I will not reward myself until I have lost 20 pounds is not as effective as 5 pound loss rewards. I am sure that you have heard it said that inch by inch is hard in doing something but yard by yard is hard.
- If when you are dieting, headache pain comes on before meals, or when you have skipped a meal entirely, the cause could be low blood sugar brought on by an inadequate amount of protein and carbohydrate in your daily intake.
- Fish, cheese, and meat are good sources of protein.
- Try eating six mini meals instead of three regular ones.
- Do not eat hot dogs on your diet. Sometimes they cause headaches because of the food additives such as sodium nitrate and nitrite processors.
- Headaches could be caused also by too strenuous an exercise program. The smaller blood vessels do not expand fast enough to accommodate the stepped up blood flow and headache pain comes on. The solution is to slow down.
- When you begin to diet, some sleepless nights may occur because a change in eating habits sometimes upsets the body's blood sugar causing an inability to fall asleep. If this happens try taking a walk, or you might try making yourself a warm milk drink which is conducive to sleep. Other favorite drinks to help this problem are the herbal teas such as camomile and catnip.
- If you do not have enough carbohydrates in your diet, it will make you tired because your body is forced to burn up too many necessary fats. Prevent this by eating carbohydrates, proteins and vitamin B. A glass of orange juice is a great pick me upper.
- Keep a diet diary to log your eating habits. Be very honest and use this diary to determine the best steps to take in keeping on a weight loss program.
- Many people believe that liquids do not count in calories on a diet. Tea and coffee are relatively free of calories but fruit juices, soft drinks, and alcohol are not and they are really add up to the days total.
- Weight loss can be very dramatic the first couple of weeks that you go on the diet and then can plateau or cease entirely. Exercise can carry you off a plateau.
- Many times eating is a way of coping with some situation in life. The next time that you have a case of the blues instead of reaching for food, reach for the telephone instead and make an appointment for something like a manicure, facial, or new hair style.
- No one every loses weight unless they really want to and have determined in their mind that they are going to reach their goal. It doesn't matter what anyone says or

how many helpful tips one gets, unless they are psychologically ready to diet, it usually is fruitless.

- If you are someone who needs encouragement to get those added pounds off, join a help group such as weight watchers.
- Do not feel resentful of another person who seems to be able to eat anything and not gain, but realize everyone's metabolism is different and accept yourself as you are.
- When you are cooking dinner, chew sugarless gum or even hold a toothpick in your mouth to remind you not to taste the food.
- Get some support. Exchange low calorie recipes with friends or walk with someone in the mornings or evenings who has the same goal.
- Many times we eat just because it is time to eat. This may call for a life style change such as doing something different on your break from work rather than eating. If it is hard to say no to the doughnuts at that time, try taking a walk in the fresh air.
- Some experts say to try and picture yourself as you want to be. Imagine yourself a thinner person and think how you will look in a new knit dress etc. They say that getting rid of your fat image will help you keep weight off.
- Sometimes people use food as a substitute for affection. Getting a friendly hug and some self image food can sometimes soothe those that have the snack feelings.
- Don't just hope you can lose weight, but if you set your mind to something and believe you can do it you can. To just hope you can do something is self defeating. Get some determination and belief in yourself.
- Do not get discouraged if you slip once in awhile. Everyone fails occasionally but it is not a reason to give up and go back to your old ways of eating or skipping your exercise regime.
- This sounds pretty simplistic but eat less fat and sugar and eat more vegetable, fruits, and grains.
- Avoid or limit your alcohol intake.
- Try sneaking some exercise into your day by standing instead of sitting, walking quickly instead of shuffling along, and use the stairs instead of the elevator or escalator.
- Learn to be assertive enough to say no thank you to those that insist you eat more.
- Turn down second helpings and rich desserts.
- Learn to slow down and relax and it may help you to prevent that automatic eating response when you feel frazzled. Close your eyes and imagine a peaceful scene.
- Some people are going to be fighting extra weight all of their lives and they need to come to terms with that fact and that they will permanently have to change their life style of eating.
- They say that sunflower and sesame seeds improve the memory and powers of concentration.
- Yo yo dieting with ones weight going up and down is worse than maintaining a consistent weight even if it is a little more than we should have.
- Some people recklessly start on miracle diets with no consideration for the nutritional value and end up poorly nourished and in a less than good state of health.

- Be aware of the diets that are dangerous because the limited number of nutrients eventually cause the body to take the nutrients that it needs from its own cells.
- Orange juice is good for quick energy and loaded with vitamin C but be aware that it is also loaded with calories.
- Many of the experts believe that if you eat your food too rapidly, your nervous system will not have time to warn you when you are full so try eating slowly or chew longer or take smaller bites.
- There is a thin line between exercising the will power necessary to stay slim and totally depriving yourself of the food you enjoy. If you never indulge yourself, life can seem pretty grim. If this is one of your problems, try eating a small piece of cake once a week or so.

If you start to give up sweets, then after awhile anything that is sweet will begin to be too sweet for you.

- Try to make a rule not to eat after 6 p.m.. Generally speaking your body does not have time to burn up the extra calories before you go to sleep.
- Try substituting quality for quantity in food. When you are eating less perhaps you can afford the less fatty cut of meat such as a filet mignon instead of a more fat laden piece of meat.
- Fish is one of the best main stays of a person trying to lose or maintain weight so get yourself a recipe book with some good fish dishes in it and add this to your menu.
- One key to successful dieting is your ability to shake the salt habit. Salt helps you retain fluid.
- Guilt can play havoc with our self image when we feel we are not doing enough or trying hard enough. Do not let guilt rob you of what you have accomplished because no routine or regimen is right for everyone. In other words, beauty and fitness do not have to be an all or nothing proposition. For instance for a woman who has never exercised at all, working up to 15 minutes of exercise four times a week can be a big hurdle.
- Think big but start small. One new make up trick, one new exercise may be all you can handle at the moment.
- Just start doing something because when we do nothing we feel guilty and that is defeating. Sometimes doing all the things we need or think we should do become over whelming so we do nothing.
- It has been said that most diets do not work. It is not a diet that gets the weight off but a way of eating that can be incorporated into a lifestyle as a way of life and not as a dogmatic regimen.
- If you have been losing weight, then treat yourself to a new outfit, and the compliments that you get will inspire you to continue.
- If you will store all of your favorite cakes, cookies, and other goodies in non see through containers in inaccessible place, it will help curb your sweet tooth. Another deterrent to eating these kind of treats is to make the package difficult to open. Staple the potato chips bags and cookie bags closed.

- Yogurt will help you keep calcium in your diet, so eat a cup a day. Women need at least 1000 milligrams of calcium daily beginning in their teens and 20's.
- When dieting, begin to take control of your eating habits and that is at the supermarket.
- Plan ahead so you can shop for foods thoughtfully with a list that you do not deviate from.
- Never go grocery shopping with an empty stomach
- It is very important to cut down on fats in our diet not only for weight control but for our heart health also.
- One idea is that it is not only what you eat that makes the difference but when you eat it and in what combinations. This when and how factor is the missing link that insures success in losing weight and maintaining it.
- The continuous eating of the wrong things will eventually result in some kind of disease. It is much easier to prevent something that try to cure it.
- Our bodies are 70% water so we should be eating a diet that is high in water content. This includes fruit and vegetables which should be predominate in the diet. The other 30% can be foods that are concentrated such as breads, meat, dairy products, and grains.
- Weight loss on crash diets is usually water rather than fat. As soon as your body readjusts its water balance, you will be right back where your started.
- Crash or fad diets also do not help your eating habits which need to be changed for a consistent weight loss and keeping it off.
- Slow and steady weight loss give you time to discover your own weaknesses and strengths in relation to food and gives your body time to adjust.
- Even low calorie food is fattening in large quantities.
- Starvation is not a diet and cutting back on food to the subsistence level or skipping meals entirely is not wise because not only does it lower your metabolism but when you do eat, you will have a tendency to eat more.
- Fat has over twice the calories than does protein or carbohydrates.
- Carrot and celery sticks can get boring even to the most dedicated vegetable eaters so try a small box of raisins or a cup of plain popcorn.
- The experts say that it takes 20 minutes for your stomach to tell your brain that you have had enough to eat. If you eat in less time, the message is not transmitted and you will still feel hungry.

STAYING ON YOUR DIET AT A PARTY

- You think someone will be offended if you do not take some of the things they have to eat when in reality they do not notice.
- If a host or hostess is continually offering you food, it is not offensive to simply say no thank you. A good host or hostess would not force someone to eat something they did not want or invite a diabetic to eat chocolate.
- Try to position yourself as far away from the food as possible. The closer you are to the snacks the easier it will be to have just a little.

- Carry around the same soda all evening and no one will even know if it is your first or second.
- If it is a dinner party, use some techniques such as eating very slowly. This way you will not have to refuse seconds.
- Deemphasize the food and concentrate on other things such as seeing friends, enjoying conversations and meeting new people.

EXERCISE

- One medical man said that you can run on adrenaline until you are 40 but after that you pay a high price for no exercise.
- If you will be faithful to an exercise regimen, whether it is jogging or walking home from work, it will pay you over and over again in the extra energy reserve it builds for you.
- Many times there does not seem to be enough time to do everything we need to does not alone what we want to do and adding an exercise regimen sometimes cuts into time we do not have. Try using your lunch time and break times for a brisk walk or even a little jogging in place.
- The common complaint of women is that the accumulations of excess fat always seem to go to the thighs. Three of the best exercises for the thighs is swimming and playing tennis, and racquetball. You use the whole leg in these sports.
- If you do not seem to have time for exercise, use all your time to advantage and stretch whenever and as often as you can. Stretching is a good exercise and all you need to do is to stand as tall as possible, lift your arms up and try to touch the ceiling with your feet remaining flat on the floor. Do this stretch at least four or five times a day and work on good posture.
- Bicycling is a good muscle exercise and a stimulant to the circulatory system. This is a good way to do something good for you as a family also.
- The person who needs the exercise routine the most are the ones who come home too exhausted to develop a routine.

WALKING

- Walking is natures way to help with excessive tension, nervous strain, anger or frustration. Try walking home from work if it is not to far and if it is safe.
- Walking helps you work off the daily tensions because you do not have to concentrate and it is natural and automatic.
- When you exercise be sure that you choose the correct shoes and what you wear is very important so choose something comfortable and lets you move with ease.
- Walking is the closest thing to a perfect exercise and it can be done by almost anybody, young and old. All it requires is a good pair of walking shoes.
- Walking is an aerobic exercise which means it get you to breathe deeply while your heart beats faster. It can lower blood pressure caused by stress and is even a natural tranquilizer which reduces anxiety and tension.
- Walking improves the muscle tone in the legs.

- A noted cardiologist said that he felt that this form of exercise provided more blood to the brain and helped people relax and think more clearly.
- Walk a specific time of day so that it gets to be a habit.
- Get your spouse to walk with you for it is a good time to spend some time together in this busy world.
- When you walk, if you stroll along slowly, stopping to talk to people or smell the flowers and then take a few more steps, you may feel relaxed at the end but you will not accomplish much in the terms of fitness.
- When you walk, swing your arms, hold your head up high and walk moving fast enough to make your breathing deep.
- You can even walk if you do not go to work. Instead of sitting down for a chat with your neighbors, ask them to go for a short walk with you around the block.
- Start thinking of places you can walk instead of riding like walking up the stairs instead of the elevator.
- When it is hot and humid, dress accordingly. The clothing should be cotton because cotton absorbs perspiration and lets the excess moisture evaporate as you walk.
- In cold weather the opposite is true. Dress with layers of clothing that trap the warm air and hold it next to your body. The more you walk, then the warmer you become.
- Pay the most attention to the type of shoe you are wearing for walking. Good walking shoes should support and cup your heel, support your arch, protect the ball of your foot, provide traction, and allow your sole to flex for each pushoff.
- A study at one University showed that a 15 minute walk reduced tension even more effectively than tranquilizers.
- Make a note of how your cat stretches to see how you should do stretch exercises. The movements are slow, easy, with no jerking movements. Extend your muscles as far as you can without jerking and then reach a little bit further.
- There is no argument that exercise should be a vital part of our lives, but what about those times when bad weather curtails this very necessary routine. Well, they say that all you really need is about 15 minutes three times a week to maintain your condition if you are in pretty good shape already. There are not too many people that cannot work a half an hour from each days schedule for some exercise if they want to.
- One good indoor exercise to keep us from getting too flabby is jumping rope. It is a good aerobic exercise that can actually burn more calories than jogging and it requires very little space and no special expensive equipment except a rope and a good pair of shoes.
- When you jump rope be sure that you jump on a surface that does not cause too much jarring to the spine. It is always good to read up on the exercise you are going to do so that injury does not occur.
- If you have stairs at your disposal, run up and down the stairs. This is tougher than running on level ground so you get a better work out.
- Be sure that you warm up and cool down before and after exercise. These are basic stretching and simple exercises.

- If you like music, turn on the radio or stereo and dance to your hearts content. Let yourself go and really move your arms and legs. This can really work up a sweat if you give it all you got.
- If you have the space and money to purchase an exercise machine like a stationery bicycle or rowing machine these can be very beneficial especially in inclement weather. When you work out on these, you can read a book or even watch TV and the time goes by real fast.
- Another exercise tool is the rebounder.
- The secret is to not let the equipment collect dust but to create a consistent workable routine that works for you.
- Everyone is different and not one specific exercise is for everyone so choose what suits your lifestyle best, but choose something.
- The principle behind warming up is to get your body going. Some good warm-ups are running in place for 3 minutes or walking up and down stairs for five minutes. Just get your heart to pumping.

GOOD TIPS FOR THE DOUBLE CHIN:

- Watch your posture and hold your head up.
- Do not read in bed with your chin down toward your collarbone.
- It is best to sleep without a pillow or a use a very flat one.
- Stick your tongue out and try to touch your nose with the tip.

FACIAL EXERCISES

- One area that people fail to exercise is the face and neck and this is where aging shows up first. Tiny muscles shape the expression of your face. They provide the underlying support structure for the skin and help keep it firm and youthful. However, no muscle remains firm without use so exercise your face muscle to keep them firm. Do not stretch the skin however.
- If you are anxious or tense, it will show on your face by setting your jaw. You will find hard to remain in this tenseness if you can laugh so try making faces at yourself.
- Laughter is a wonderful exercise for the face and body and one of the best ways of getting tummy muscles into shape.
- Crunch your face up into your nose as though you have smelled something unpleasant.
- Open your mouth and eyes as wide as you can and stick your tongue out to help your throat muscles to release and do a silent scream.
- Move your lips to the left and right and follow with the biggest grin you can muster.
- Open your eyes up wide and see if you can make the grin stretch from ear to ear.
- Tuck in your chin and pull in your lower lip and this will help firm the muscles at the front of your neck.
- Exercises for the neck are important also.
- Hold the head correctly — not too far forward or too far back because this can create tense muscles that connect the neck to the shoulders.

- Posture is one of the most important factors in keeping the neck free from tension and stiffness so check to see that you are sitting in correct posture.
- Do not forget to moisturize the neck as well as the face.
- The secret of success of any exercise program is to keep at it because the most effective exercises will do little to tone muscles and firm if stopped after a few days or a week.

WINTER EXERCISE

- To get the most body benefits out of a winter walk is to walk briskly. Most of the experts recommend that you walk at about 4 miles per hour. Check your pace by timing how long it takes you to walk l mile. Twenty city blocks equal one mile. At that speed you will burn about 300 calories an hour, begin to see your derriere and legs tighten, and improve the efficiency of your heart.
- In the winter time, warm up by walking slowly for three to five minutes and then increase your pace by taking longer strides while swinging your arms.
- Skiing is a fun exercise and it strengthens the thigh and dierrere and stomach muscles. It is very important to get in shape before you hit the slopes.
- Cross county skiing is good for the whole body and is rated one of the best aerobic sports. You will burn up about 600 calories an hour. Getting out in the country among God's creation can do wonders for stress also.
- If you do not want to spend money on buying ski equipment you can rent or a cheaper winter workout maybe just putting on a good pair of snow shoes and take an invigorating hike through the snow covered wilderness.
- Snowshoeing is not as good aerobically as cross county skiing but it helps develop leg muscles, increases your endurance, and will burn up about 400 calories an hour.
- Use water in your exercise program. When it is too hot to walk or jog, stay cool in a pool and water jog either moving around or in one place.
- To tone the arms and chest, rest the arms just beneath the water surface and push down and back as far as you can.
- Always warm up before exercising to prevent the risk of injury.

VACATION AND EXERCISE

- When you are on vacation it is harder to keep up your exercise routine so incorporate exercise into whatever you are doing.
- If you are at the beach, go swimming.
- Rent a boat and go rowing.
- Jog in the sand on the beach.
- If you are in the mountains, go for some hikes.
- Look for places that have a pool.
- Play tennis and golf.
- Of course you can always go walking but you need to know the area and do not go alone. Incorporate your walking into sightseeing. Do not ride everywhere you want to

- Exercise in your room.
- Bring some of your aerobic exercise tapes or check the TV schedule for an exercise show.
- If you will exercise after a long trip it will help to get of the effect of jet lag or fatigue from sitting in a car or on a plane for hours.
- Do your stretching exercises before sleep.
- Things do affect you when you travel like different time zones, climates, temperatures, plus various altitudes. Be sure to allow your body to adjust and not push too hard.
- Before you get out of bed in the morning, stretch like a cat. Remove the pillow if you use one, and inhale deeply on your back. Stretch each side of your body a few times as you breathe deeply so that you can get more oxygen into your blood.

CHAPTER 11

Proverbs 27:9
"Perfume and incense bring joy to the heart " NIV

"MY, YOU SMELL GOOD!" — FRAGRANCES

- One good hint for the office regarding different scents is to wear a brisk, clean fragrance and not too much. You may not be able to smell it after awhile but it may prove to be a bit much for the fellow office workers.
- A clean fragrance or soft powder will give off a pleasant smell without being intrusive.
- Crisp, soft scents are more easily associated with professionalism then the heavier scents and this goes for after shave lotions also.
- Do not apply perfume or cologne if you are going to go out in the sun to sunbathe because it may make your skin blotchy.
- Put a small amount of your favorite fragrance in your bath water.
- Put some bath oil or baby oil into your bath water with the fragrance and it will help it to last longer on the skin.
- When applying fragrances, chose your pulse points such as behind your ears, your wrists, back of the knees, and ankles.
- Be sure when you choose a fragrance that it is your personality not someone else's and makes a statement about you that you want to make.
- Try different fragrances on until you are comfortable with one and wear it for awhile before purchasing.
- There was a study done by a large fragrance firm and they found that a persons fragrance selection is affected by emotions and feeling from past experience. For in-

stance if spicy smells are your favorite scent, perhaps you had an uncle or grandfather that smoked a spicy pipe tobacco and recalls pleasant memories.

- Scents are also affected by the persons age, skin color, health and hormonal balances.
- When you a trying to decide which scent you want, do not try on more than two at a time.
- Spray or dab the scent on each wrist and at the elbow.
- Walk around the store to let the fragrance adjust to your skin chemistry.
- Do not try fragrances on a day when you are under a lot of stress or are on a special kind of diet containing low or high fat. All of these things will affect the chemistry of your body and change the fragrance.
- Extreme hot or cold temperatures will also affect the way a scent smells.
- Heat will cause a fragrance to give off a stronger scent.
- Keep your work place in mind when you are ready to buy a new fragrance.
- Perfumes are heavier than colognes and it may be best to wear the cologne at the office not the perfume.
- Your personality will cause you to lean toward certain fragrances. Extroverts may choose something more wild than an introvert.
- Many times we are attracted to someone because of the way she or he smells. Never underestimate the power of scent.
- Never try to cover up the lack of bathing with perfume or cologne because perspiration and the fragrance will give off a most unpleasant odor.
- If you wear a fragrance for months and then all of a sudden it seems to change, don't blame the perfume. It can be changed by either starting or stopping a medication or perhaps a changed diet can change the scent.
- If you become pregnant, your favorite perfume may smell differently on you.
- Any hormonal change in the body or a severe illness or operation can cause a change in the way the perfume smells on your skin.
- Since perfume is so expensive now days, do not buy the biggest bottle of a new fragrance for the first time or try buying the cologne which will not be as expensive. If it is a good fragrance, the essential scent will be exactly the same whether it is perfume or cologne. The only difference is the strength.
- If you keep the larger bottles of perfume and cologne for a long time they tend to evaporate leaving the scent stronger than you wanted.
- Keep your fragrances capped tightly and store in a darkened drawer to keep the scent from not changing.
- Wearing a good quality fragrance affects our mood.
- Know what type of perfumes to wear to what occasion. Don't wear an exotic scent first thing in the morning or a light floral cologne with an elegant evening gown. Wear the perfume that fits the time of day and the occasion.
- To use perfume correctly, do not mix the fragrances. If you can afford it, buy the soap, cologne, bath oil, powder, and perfume of your choice all in one fragrance.

- A good perfume wardrobe should include a minimum of two fragrances. One for the day time and one for the evening.
- The outdoorsy smells are best for day time and the more sophisticated romantic ones are best in the night.
- Perfume is the most highly concentrated fragrance, toilet water is next, and cologne is the lightest scent.
- Buy only a small amount of perfume at a time because it can change scent if left unused for a long time or not kept tightly capped.
- Heat and sunlight also can change the scent of a perfume so do not leave it out on your dresser where the sun can affect it.
- The experts say that keeping cologne in the refrigerator does not prolong the life — however, it feels real refreshing to splash cool cologne on especially if it is a hot day.
- Always buy good perfume. A cheap scent can really be a turn off especially in an office.
- It is best to have no fragrance at all than too much.
- The best pulse spots for perfume are front of the ears, nape of the neck, inside of the wrist, elbows and back of knees.
- The heat of the body will warm the perfume and help it to blossom.
- Do not apply perfume to your clothing or furs. It may stain.
- If perfume does not last on you, try using the perfumed lotions.
- Solid perfumes will not evaporate and will stay longer also.
- When you use spray perfumes, hold the container only 2 inches away from your body so that the full impact of the mist is on your body not in the air.
- No perfume smells exactly the same on two different women. It is the body chemistry that determines the scent.
- There is nothing wrong with having a perfume that is your signature to others, but do not get so narrow in your choice that you do not wear a variety of perfumes to suit different seasons and moods.
- Get it clear in your mind what fragrances you like and dislike before you buy. Perhaps you like musk scents or floral scents but generally speaking you will tend toward a certain type and will be most happy wearing them.
- Do not try more than two different perfumes on your skin at a time. The scents will mix and not be true.
- The wearer of a perfume or cologne should give off an agreeable atmosphere for others to enjoy.
- As the temperature rises, a perfume aroma becomes stronger so a scent that smelled great in February could be too overpowering by July or August.
- The woodsy and flower scents are very nice smells for the summer.
- When the days are hot, use talcum powder or dusting powder on your arms, neck, and shoulders to give you a feel of luxury.
- Powders are also great for tired feet.
- When you buy perfume be sure that you check the seal to be sure that it has not been broken.

- If you buy perfume and the scent stays to pungent, then it is probably not suitable for daytime wear. If you like the scent, purchase it in cologne which would not be a heavy.
- If you are afraid that the perfume may evaporate, it will if you do not cap it tightly or if you leave it on your dressing room table. To help this problem, divide the perfume and with a small funnel and transfer some into a small clean bottle for immediate use and seal up the rest with paraffin drops of wax from a lighted candle and put it around the stopper. Then store the bottle in its box in a cool dark place.
- Heat and sunlight drastically affect the scent of a perfume.
- Perfumes will not last as long on a woman who has a dry skin so rub some natural oil on your body to help make a perfume application last longer.
- Perfume lotions will last longer on your skin also. They are not only skin softening but carry a wonderful scent.
- Sachets are a form of scent that is both subtle and long lasting. They come in a side variety of fragrances and in several forms such as cream, roll on, compacts and talcum.
- Purse perfumes are a nice addition to your fragrance collection and usually have containers that are easily refillable. Also, most companies make a solid perfume in stick, compact, or roll on form which is designed especially for handbag and travel. They are so nice to refresh yourself on a trip.

MAKING YOUR HOME AND CAR SMELL FRAGRANT

- Use your favorite fragrances in candles in your home or even a spray from the bottle will give your home an inviting aura.
- Don't forget to spritz a small amount on your pillow.
- You could even shake a small amount into the car cushion
- Add some to your window curtains for further refreshing smell throughout the house.
- You can put a soft subtle perfume in your drawers by using sachets or tiny drops of your favorite perfume put on with your hand.
- Potpourri is a great way to add some romance and elegance to your home especially on special holidays like Christmas but they wonderful ones for all year round now.
- Get some hanging fragrant pomander balls and hang in your kitchen to mask all sorts of unpleasant odors. You can use a lemon, lime or the traditional orange as a base and insert whole cloves all the way around making sure that the cloves are very close together. Add some pretty ribbon and hang in the kitchen. The ball will shrink with time but the scent will still remain.
- Try creating an herbal odor with basil, mints, thyme, or rosemary and plant them in a recycled egg carton or what ever you wish to plant them in and put them in a window sill.
- Scented candles are wonder and they have them in many of the favorite perfumes now.
- Try putting a drop of your favorite perfume on a cold light bulb. When you turn the light on the fragrance will slowly spread throughout the entire room.

- Mint gives a wonderful odor and if you put a bunch in water in a pretty jar, the odor will sift throughout the room.
- At Christmas time or any time for that matter, a nice fragrance is the mixture of cedar chips and pine needles.
- Take all your special scented guest soaps and fill a pretty dish or basket with them in a guest bath or put them in your lingerie drawer.
- Use the sample fragrance cards that come from department stores to give you a special fragrance in your drawers or in between sheets or towels.
- If you leave books out for show, spritz a scent on a book mark and let it hold your place and give a fresh smell to the room.
- Your scent is one way that people remember you so choose your scent carefully.
- Sprinkle some fragrant bath powder between your sheets.
- If you would like the woodsy and floral scents to permeate your home, spray the air-conditioner to cool the air and refresh it at the same time.
- Scented candles are great to use during the hot summer months to keep your home smelling refreshed.
- Candles create a mood of serenity and peace. I had a friend that once told me I needed to slow down and she bought me a candle and said, "You can't walk fast past a candle." I never forgot that and candles are one of my favorite things.

CHAPTER 12

Psalm 63:4
" and in your name I will lift up my hands."
NIV

DON'T LOOK NOW BUT YOUR HANDS, FEET, AND TEETH ARE SHOWING

Strong beautiful nails are a big fashion statement and the artificial nail business is booming because so many women cannot grow their own.

HAND CARE

- Use a hand cream frequently when it is cold and keep an extra container in the desk at work and another in your handbag.
- Another good place to keep hand moisturizer is in your car so if you forget it will be handy in the car.
- Moisturize hands as often as possible.
- Every once in awhile it is good to coat your hands with a good moisturizer and sleep with gloves to keep the moisturizer in. Try using baby oil.
- Hands complete your look of grooming. Graceful hand movements add to the look of a poised individual.

- Talking with your hands is fine but an over abundance of movement could be distracting but nevertheless the experts say that talking with your hands is a positive sign.
- If your hands get stiff and tired during the day, give them some exercise. Stretch your fingers out as far as you can reach. Then make a tight fist with each hand and repeat this procedure several times. Then shake your hands from the wrists and pretend you are playing the piano in the air. This is make your hands feel more relaxed and pick up your workday.
- Remove super glue from your hands by soaking the glue with nail polish remover.
- Our hands are seen just about as much as our faces and it is our hands that tell others how we see and care about ourselves. It is the total look of grooming that completes the finished touch that says I care about myself.
- Hands are a real age give away so use a lot of moisturizer and sunscreen.
- When you age, the hands are one area that gives away your age if they are not taken care of in a proper manner.
- If you have extremely dry hands and are having a hard time getting them back into shape, put some petroleum jelly all over your hands at night and sleep with some white gloves on. By morning your hands will be much smoother.
- You do not get your hands, skin or hair in condition in ten minutes or even ten days. It takes working at it all the time and it takes planning.
- A tan looks nice with the light shades of nail polishes. They will create a contrast with your tan.
- Weathered and wrinkled hands will look softer with the frosted shades and frosted nail polishes also make shorter nails look longer. The word here is soft colors so it does not draw attention to the hand.
- It takes frequent creaming and moisturizing of the hands to keep them soft and pretty when the weather is cold.

NAIL CARE

- Check your diet to see that it contains enough vitamin A and of course adequate protein.
- Prevent dryness of the nail by protecting your hands from the elements.
- The excessive and repeated use of polishes, nail hardeners and removers all dry the nails.
- Some polish removers contain acetone which is a powerful solvent and is very drying to the nails. There are some polish removers on the market now that do not have the harshness of acetone and will say so on the label.
- Even the hardest and well cared for nails will break if they are used as tools such as prying off lids.
- The artificial nails today are much tougher and more sophisticated than ever before and the methods used are less likely to damage the nail underneath.
- Be sure that you go to a trained and reputable manicurist. The do it yourself sets are not as good and the nails are precast so they tend to look unnatural and also the glue

is often too weak to ensure adhesion. A good manicurist can apply and file the nails to look like your own.

- There is more interest than ever in the artificial nail or nail tip. Nail tips are good because they allow your nail to breathe and they simply grow out with your natural nail.
- Before beginning a garden project, dig your nails into a bar of soap and they will clean up much better and faster. Better yet wear a pair of gardening gloves.
- Nails are made of protein and they grow from the skin rather than muscle or bone.
- It takes about six months for a nail to grow from bottom to top and as we get older the growth gets slower.
- Do not mistreat your nails. Use a pencil to dial the telephone rather than the finger.
- There are many theories for nail health — one of them being that Knox gelatin whether eaten or applied does not seem to help as they first thought but there is increasing evidence that the addition of zinc to the diet does.
- There may be a link between strong teeth and strong nails. However, a beauty plan that benefits your entire body will work for teeth and nails alike.
- If you have the nail biting habit, you will be less likely to continue if you keep your nails nicely manicured or if you wear artificial nails, it is virtually impossible to continue the habit.
- There are some good nail hardeners on the market that may help the splitting of your nails.
- Never use nails as substitute plier or screwdrivers.
- Flaking and peeling nails are generally symptoms of excessive strain on the nail or an excessive amount of dryness.
- If you clip your nails, be sure you always follow the nails natural curve.
- If you clip or file the sides of your nails, this will encourage chipping.
- If you have nails that break off and peel, then your nail may be too dry. Purchase a good product that will put oil back into your nail and you will find that you can grow your nails longer with less breakage.
- It is important to not neglect your nails on both your hands and feet because over exposure to water and heat will dry them out causing cracks and peeling.
- Some wonderful products are out now that add oil to your nails that help keep them from peeling cracking and breaking.
- A couple of good products that you might consider is a nail oil called DeLore which is a natural nail oil and Redken also puts out a good nail and cuticle oil.
- There are many others also, so consult your beautician who usually has a person doing nails in their shops.ng and peeling.
- You can soak your nails in oil as well as add a good nail oil which can be purchased from your beautician.
- Wear rubber gloves when you do dishes.
- Always use a good hand cream.
- Rub a special cuticle cream into your cuticles an nails can help cracking around the cuticle.
- Nails that get stained or discolored tips.

- Clean by using lemon juice on a cotton swab rubbing for two or three minutes. Then rinse the solution off, dry the nails and buff.
- Do not apply nail polish directly to the nail but use an under coat first.
- If you have a lot of nail problems, check out your eating habits as well as your hand habits such as how you dial a phone, work in your garden and just how you neglect your nails.
- Don't use your nails as tools.
- Eat correctly
- Some of the nails worst enemies are dialing a phone, typing, filing, housework, and opening soda pop cans just to name a few.
- Begin to be aware of how you are abusing your nails and take some measures to stop.
- You could wear gloves around the home and for gardening.
- Nail biting is a sign of nervousness and can reflect negatively for your image.
- Another negative is the brittle damaged nails that are unkempt.
- They say that right handed people have a faster nail growth on their right hands.
- People who type and stimulate the finger tips have nails that grow faster. Whether they stay that way after they have grown out a little is a matter of care.
- Wear rubber gloves for your work chores that involve water and when you garden.
- A lack of the mineral zinc can show up as white spots on the nails. Try adding brewer's yeast to your diet or add seafood on a weekly basis. The spots will not disappear but will grow out with the nail as you make them more healthy.
- You may get spots on your fingernails just because of the wear and tear they endure or even overvigorous manicuring. You rarely see these spots on toenails that are better protected.
- Dry brittle nails are more commonly caused by abuse than by any specific deficiency in the diet.
- Nails need extra care in the cold, so keep a pair of gloves handy when you are going out in inclement weather.
- Massage nails and cuticles with a lubricating cream often.
- Some things that dry out the nails and weaken them are detergents, glues, paint strippers and other cleaning chemicals.
- If you spend a lot of time in the water , it will take its toll on improperly protected nails. Water leeches out your natural nail moisture and makes them brittle.
- Just as water lifts off dirt, it also lifts off the top layers of your nails and causes polish to lose its sheen.

MANICURE

- Make a good manicure a once a week project and then help your manicure to last all week by simply applying a top coat each day. This seals in the polish and protects the nails.
- It is usually best to file than clip the nail.
- One factor that determines the lasting ability of your manicure is the freshness of your polish.

- For extra protection for polished nails that chip off on the ends, polish the back of the nail tips. This reduces the exposed surface area of the nail and strengthens the nail tips.
- Always conclude the manicure with a good top coat and put it on every other day to keep your manicure looking fresh.
- If you will file your nail a little more square than the oval that goes too far into the side of the nail, it minimize breakage and is still flattering even on short nails.
- Use a diamond deb file or an emery board. The metal file is hard on the nails.
- Treat your nails to a warm oil bath and massage the cuticle to stimulate circulation.
- Be sure you remove all oil from the nail before applying polish.
- The tips of the nails should be very smooth.
- If you want your nail polish to stay on longer, try putting a coat of clear polish on top and tip of nails each night.
- To stimulate growth of your nail, try massaging nails and tips as often as possible to increase circulation to the fingers.
- Whenever it is convenient, massage your fingers and hands to keep them flexible.
- Nails look best a little shorter and always manicured and polished subtly If you have older looking hands any bright nail polish will draw attention to them.
- It is best to apply 2-3 thin coats of polish than one heavy coat of polish.
- Grooming our nails is the final touch for the total groomed look and probably one of the most neglected.
- Even if you do not like to wear polish, nails and hands should be well groomed with proper filing, cleansing, and moisturizing.
- It takes planning and time to see that your chipped nail polish is repaired or to even get the polish on in the first place.
- Keep the tools that you use for filing your nails and buffing etc. in good condition.
- Make sure that your scissors, or nail clippers are not dull.
- Learn to pamper your nails because they are an important part of your total look.
- Dip newly painted nails into ice water to make the polish dry quickly and evenly.
- Use a nail polish remover that will not dry out the nails. Use one with the least alcohol in it and states acetone free on the label.
- They say that nail enamels will be smooth and ready to use if you store them in the refrigerator.
- Use a good cuticle cream and massage good into the finger tips.

FOOT CARE

- In the summer when we wear so many open toe shoes and sandals it is imperative for you to have a good pedicure.
- To make feet look smaller, try a subtle shade of polish like a smoky rose.
- Women with bony feet or heavily veined feet should always polish with soft colors.
- Slenderize chubby toes with frosted shades.
- The feet have two main functions. They support the body and propel us in walking. What happens to your feet affects your whole body including your posture and also

your disposition. Most of us neglect our feet when they are tucked away in boots and pumps during the winter and suddenly during warm weather they are on display. With a little time and attention you can look your loveliest right down to your toes.

- Feet change and continue to change so a shoe that fit you fine at one time may not feel as good anymore.
- Feet can elongate or spread particularly if you are on your feet a lot or you are overweight.
- An all purpose talcum put on your feet will help to absorb moisture.
- When wearing socks in tennis shoes, be sure that they are all cotton.
- Puffiness in the feet and ankles is often caused by pressure on the veins at the back of the knee and is a complaint often given by secretaries who sit with crossed legs for long periods of time. Try changing your position at work and getting your feet up in the air for a few minutes. Also, it is best not to cross the legs at any time because of the pressure it puts on the back of the leg causing varicose veins and incorrect posture.
- One beauty aid that they have out now for spider veins in the legs is a water proof leg makeup that comes in a tube. Things that cause these small blood vessels to break are having many children and prolonged standing. Consult your doctor if they are large and unsightly.
- In the summer time with all the open-toed shoes as well as going barefoot at the beach and pool, it is important to have a pedicure. You can keep you toes looking nice if you have a pedicure about every 10 days.
- One area that gets hard and unsightly in the summertime is the heel of the foot. When this happens take a pumice stone to the shower with you and lightly rub the pumice stone over the bottom of the heel to give it a smoother look.
- To freshen overworked feet soak them in ice water. This reduces any swelling also.
- When purchasing shoes, buy them at the end of the day when the feet are the most swollen. This is one way to make sure that the shoes will not pinch later on.
- Use fashion footwear to make the most of your feet. For example if you have long narrow feet with slim ankles, choose a pair of sandals with the ankle straps to make your feet a real fashion touch.
- If you have thick ankles, then the simple thong sandals would be best.
- If you have your feet beautifully manicured and you have pretty ankles, show off one of your good features with a delicate ankle bracelet.
- If you will buy shoes with various heel heights, it will put pressure on different parts of the foot and leg depending on how high a heel you wear.
- Your tired feet will feel so good if you take time to soak them, so sit on the edge of the tub with your feet under the faucet and turn the water on full blast. Start with warm water and gradually increase to a little hotter. Then after a few minutes, cool the water down again and dry your feet with a cotton towel.
- A good massage and rub down of the feet will do wonders.
- Many salons that do manicures will do pedicures also if you do not wish to do this yourself.

- After soaking your feet do not forget to push back the cuticles and clean under the toenails.
- When you massage your feet, include your legs and use a cream or lotion to stimulate circulation. Be sure all the lotion residue is wiped off the toenails before you polish.
- Spray your favorite scent on your feet.
- Remember to use subtle shades if you want to make big feet look smaller.
- Use bold tones of polish if you want to show off your toes.
- To keep your feet the healthiest, wear clean hosiery each day and add a touch of talcum powder to the inside of your shoes each morning to keep both shoes and feet fresh.
- Give your shoes times to air out by rotating the pair you wear each day.
- For tired feet, soak them in lukewarm water with one cup of cider vinegar.
- For warm weather, soft leather and fabric shoes are the best.

PEDICURE

- Begin by giving your feet a good soaking in warm suds.
- Scrub thoroughly with a soft brush.
- Cut the toenails straight across instead of rounding them off.
- Smooth the edges of the nails with an emery board using the coarse side of the board. The fine side is for finishing.
- Remove the rough skin from the heels with a lotion formulated to remove calloused areas or try a wet pumice stone buffing lightly.
- Put cotton between the toes and polish with two coats of thin polish.
- When feet are uncovered they are looked at like our hands so make this a part of your total grooming routine.
- Corn starch makes a terrific foot powder.
- Make sure that your feet are free of moisture before putting on stockings and shoes and sprinkle a little talcum powder between the toes and on the soles of your feet.
- To keep your heels and feet soft and smooth, rub on moisturizing cream preferably one that contains lanolin at night and this will help you not to get cracks on the heels.
- Another foot tip for real dry skin on the feet, is to apply a generous amount of petroleum jelly or baby oil before bedtime and cover them with cotton socks and go to sleep. In the morning your feet will be silky soft.

TEETH

- A lovely smile is one of the most important beauty assets but many people do not smile because they are ashamed of their teeth.
- Some of the beauty experts say that when a person smiles, their beauty quotient goes up 50%.
- A smile projects warmth, understanding, or love and illuminates the face like no make up can.
- Do not use harsh products on your teeth such as some whiteners which will be damaging to your tooth enamel.

- Natural tooth colors range from white to ivory and some have definite yellowish and even gray casts.
- Do not use your teeth to bite off thread, chew on pencils, crack nuts or bite bones, hard candy, or small pieces of ice. This can cause little notches in the front teeth.
- If you have always wanted to have your teeth straightened, then do it. There are many adults that have been ashamed of their teeth all of their lives that are finally doing something about it. Teeth are responsible for the contour of a face making it look young or old. If this has been a problem, see your orthodontist and you will never have to cover up a smile again with your hand.
- If you have braces on your teeth, draw attention away from your mouth to your eyes with nice make up and an attractive hairstyle, and stay away from bright shades of lipstick. A soft pink or coral lipstick would be best.
- Don't be self conscious about your braces because you will be admired for your determination to improve your appearance.
- Some of the things that discolor the teeth are great amounts of tea and coffee with out rinsing your mouth or brushing afterwards.
- Cigarette smoking is another cause of discoloration of teeth. Be sure that you brush and have the teeth cleaned frequently.
- Achieving and maintaining a dental hygiene program should require almost as much time and attention as your make up application does.
- One of the many enemies of your teeth is sugar. It joins with the bacteria in your mouth to form acid and plaque that eats your teeth and gums away. Be sure to clean your teeth as soon as possible after eating sugar and eat a lot of crunchy fibrous raw fruits and vegetables which help to clean the teeth.
- Some toothpastes that have special tooth whiteners have proven to be too harsh on the enamel.
- For a cheaper way to whiten your teeth, brush once a week with baking soda in addition to your regular brushing.
- Use toothpastes with fluoride.
- It is important to prevent the buildup of plaque for you to use dental floss. Your toothbrush cannot remove all the food particles from between the teeth and close to the gums. Flossing prevents gum disease more effectively than any other form of home dental care.
- Do not just see your dentist when you have a toothache but checkups are extremely important and teeth should be cleaned two times a year.
- It has been said the most important form of non verbal communication is the facial expression and the most important body language on the face is the smile. If you think about the people you know with and without smiles, the ones that have a smile are more attractive and make your feel better because of their response to you. Why not smile at someone for no reason and make their day.
- Do not forget to brush your tongue while you are brushing your teeth.

CHAPTER 13

Lev. 26:13
" ... I broke the bars of your yoke and enabled you to walk with heads heald high." NIV

PUT YOUR BEST FOOT FORWARD WITH GOOD POSTURE

One area that really adds to your appearance and beauty is your posture. Good posture is a beautiful carriage and the benefits are an appearance of confidence, personality and good grooming. It also is an aid to healthy body functioning, improves speech because the lungs and diaphragm have room to function properly, and gives a youthful appearance. When someone enters a room slouched over with their head down it automatically gives an aura of age, so keep your head up and walk with a gait that shows health and happiness and you will look and feel younger.

Good posture creates an illusion of beauty. Walk and sit tall.

SOME REASONS FOR BAD POSTURE:

- Lack of posture instruction in the informative years.
- Bad habits. You have had bad posture for years and need to work on some bad habits by changing them to good habits.
- Soft chairs and mattresses can cause bad posture.
- Not taking the time to walk and stand correctly will result in poor muscle tone.
- Starting to correct your posture
- Practice correct reaching and stooping which keeps your back straight. Reach forward or stoop downward to pick up something by bending your body at the hip and the knee sockets while keeping your back straight.
- Be taller and slimmer by standing against a wall in good posture and then walk. See if you can keep the feeling of a straight back.
- Good posture gives off an illusion of beauty that gives off a positive or negative message.
- Hold in your abdominal muscles.
- Your legs should swing easily from the hip joints when you walk.
- Poor nutrition and poor posture go hand in hand. Poor nutrition weakens the muscles and connective tissue so that poor posture results and if you have poor posture, it deprives the muscles of the circulation that would bring them the nutrition needed.
- Posture delivers a message which says much about how the person feels about himself.
- The three heavy sections of your body should be squarely over each other. The right carriage not only makes your body its most beautiful but also its most efficient.
- Proper balance and movement decrease body fatigue about 80%.
- Proper posture can whittle away pounds in appearance and give you the firm upward lines that are more youthful rather than the sagging lines of age.
- Your outlook on life is tied to the way that you carry yourself. When you are weighted down with worries, then you posture tends to look like how you feel.
- If you will lift the body upward, straighten your shoulders and hold your head up when you depressed or discouraged, it will help your spirits to lift also.
- When you are standing it is important to keep the weight equally distributed so stand with your feet pointing straight head and not too far apart with the weight distributed evenly between them. When you put more weight on one foot, you tend to swing your body left or right and it immediately takes you out of proper body alignment.
- The arms should fall loosely and comfortably at the sides with the elbows slightly bent.
- Pull in your abdomen, straighten the lower back, and tuck in your derriere.
- Keep your head up, pull up your rib cage, relax and drop your shoulders.
- These tips are going to take an awareness of how you are actually carrying yourself and taking some action to change some very bad habits to goods ones. When you are aware of the things you do wrong then you can begin to change them. Many backaches are the result of sitting and standing incorrectly.

- Walk toward a mirror so you can see some bad habits.
- Many times a lovely woman destroys her whole look of beauty by sitting incorrectly. Poise is lost if she sits with her lower limbs wrapped around the chair or even if she twists her legs into an awkward position.
- Be aware of what you look like when sitting with the knees not kept together.
- Many times others are drawn to us by our body language.
- It is possible to look 1/2" thinner in the waist by standing correctly.
- Here are some questions to ask yourself to become aware of your own personal posture:
- Is there an S shaped curve in the small of your back?.
- Does your chin jut out or it tucked down and back or do you tilt it upward?
- Do you see a dowagers hump beginning at the base of your neck from jutting your head forward?
- Are your shoulders tense and sometimes hunched forward and making your neck tense?
- Is the part of your back just below your neck straight or slightly curved?
- Do you have a pot belly no matter how thin you seem to get?
- Do your arms hang in the front of your body rounding your shoulders?
- If you answered yes to any of these questions you need to check your posture. If your shoulders and head are not held in a straight line, your back won't be straight either and the abdomen starts to pooch out. If we use incorrect posture for a long period of time, sometimes some parts of our body become deformed such as the dowager's hump. Guard against stooping in old age by correcting your posture now and being sure that you get enough calcium.
- Bad posture can cause back pain and headaches and can impair our breathing.
- Ballet is excellent to help poor posture. Any kind of dance training that strengthens your supporting muscles will be beneficial to your posture.
- Other beneficial things to build strong bodies and encourage better body alignment is swimming and aerobics.
- Good posture gives you a more positive self image. Begin observing posture in people and think in your mind how they come across when they have correct alignment or what kind of image is portrayed by someone with their head down and shoulders stooped.
- Try closing your eyes and imagine that you are being pulled by a string from the top of your head. This should make your whole body lengthen and straighten.
- We talk so much about clothes, hair style and makeup and neglect a very important beauty aid and that is our posture.
- How are you sitting when you are reading this book. Were your shoulders in line with each other, your back straight, and held up or were you slumping forward with your neck curved and your spine rounded and one shoulder higher than the other?
- Most people once into their teens and often before that stand, sit and even rest incorrectly.

- Examine your weak points and be aware of how to correct them and do it each and every day until you do not have to think about it again.
- Good posture will do much to preserve your muscles and joints from the wear and tear of the advancing years.
- How you hold your head influences the position of the vertebrae not only at the neck but also all the way down the spine.
- If you hold the neck in a set and rigid manner, it can lead to shortened and strained neck muscles and lead to tension headaches and even migraines.
- You can free tension by holding your head correctly.
- Aches and pains in the upper back can be caused by holding the shoulder incorrectly.
- Bring your shoulders level by standing with your weight evenly balanced on both feet and holding your head in a central position and bring your arms back at your sides. This will pull you into proper body alignment.
- The way we walk shows our poise and beauty. High heeled shoes pitch the body forward on to your toes and causes your hips to rotate inwards to compensate for the unnatural angle of the feet so it is best to wear a moderate or low heeled shoe for everyday use.
- I heard a noted obstetrician say that if women would learn to correct their posture and let their organs sit where they should, there would be less female problems later in life.
- Putting good posture rules into practice take determination and a committed effort.
- When you are standing, walking or running, your ankles should be slightly flexed to take the weight of your body and to act as shock absorbers.

CHAPTER 14

Proverbs 15:4
"The tongue that brings healing is a tree of life ..." NIV

HOW DO YOU SOUND TODAY?

Your voice is one of the most important reflections that you project to another person. It is important in all areas of your life whether just speaking in conversation or giving a speech. You can get the most expensive clothes, hairdo and make up and really look like you are put together but once you open your mouth it will say a lot about you and the way you feel about yourself.

- Your voice should project authority, control, and self confidence.
- A voice that shows confidence is not too high nor too low, too loud nor too soft, is distinct and is not a monotone.
- A lower pitched voice is easier to listen to than one that is too high.
- Use a tape recorder and tape your telephone conversations and play back the recording. This will be a help to catch words like um, UH, and you knows and other words you do not even realize you are saying. It will also give you an idea how many times you say them which can be an annoying habit when repeated too often.
- Another area to listen for is if you are pronouncing words correctly and if you are leaving the endings off of your words such as the ings.
- Listen for any nasal sound like you are talking through your nose.

- Check your rate of speech. Are you speaking too quickly or too slowly and do you need to enunciate your words correctly.
- To test your self to see if you sound nasal, pinch your nose and say Donald Duck and then say it again. There should be no difference with the nose pinched or not.
- Consciously try to lower your voice so that your voice does not sound shrill.
- If your voice sounds breathy, learn to take deep breaths that will fill your lungs. Practice reading a sentence without taking a breath.
- For a shallow sounding voice, try speaking from the diaphragm and use your lung power not just your mouth and throat.
- Be aware of any monotone sounding in your voice and if this is a problem, try singing in the shower to help with voice variety.
- Your voice should add to your image not subtract from it.
- Sometimes its just an awareness of what we sound like to be able to begin to correct it.
- Speak into the crease of a magazine to test your voice for tone quality.
- When speaking, do you clear your throat constantly.
- Do you slur over words?
- Try reading aloud to improve your voice. Use poetry or prose and listen to recordings of fine actors and actresses who speak pleasantly.
- Gracious body movements and a pleasant voice are important in presenting a pleasant image.
- Learning to relax when you speak is a big help especially relaxation of the lips, tongue and jaw.
- Speaking in public is one of the biggest fears and the only way to get over this fear is to know your material well, be confident of your voice, and do it over and over again until you realize that you do a good job at it.
- If you are serious about wanting to improve your oratory ability and your voice, it might be a good idea for you to take lessons from a voice teacher or join Toastmistress clubs.
- At least be aware of how you sound to others because it can cloud a whole picture of loveliness.
- Practice speaking to small groups and work up to larger ones. Even if you never have the goal of being a speaker, your voice still needs to be pleasant in ordinary conversation.
- Allow warmth to come through in your speaking tone and an excitement and sparkle in your eyes which conveys love to your audience. If you do this then you will be able to win them over and will automatically make your speech more acceptable.

CONVERSATION

- The next time that you are in the presence of someone who starts to gossip, change the subject immediately.
- Idle talk and mischievous tattle tales are hurtful to others and it is easy to fall into a trap when we are conversing with someone, so immediately counteract the negative

with something positive about someone. I always wonder what gossipers say about me when I am not there.

- Be very aware of the people in your circle and make every effort to draw them into the conversation.
- It is impolite to whisper or giggle when someone else is speaking. This can apply to a larger audience such as a speaker to someone teaching a Sunday school class.
- We can learn to become good conversationalist by talking to others at every opportunity. This includes the gas station attendant, clerks, and those we come in contact with everyday. The more we practice the easier it becomes.
- The best way to get someone to talk is to ask them questions about themselves.
- Do not monopolize the conversation with the letter I or me. This tends to become boring and irritating.
- A good conversationalist will be a good listener and not just hear words but really hear what the person is saying.
- Learning to converse takes two so a balance of talking and listening will make you more interesting.
- Do not get in the habit of interrupting or finishing someone else's sentence.
- Some people think that if they never say anything they will not put their foot in their mouths but that type of person is boring.
- Always establish eye contact but do not stare.
- Listen actively as others talk by keeping our eyes focused on the speaker so that they know they have our complete attention.
- When we actively listen to another person we get something from the other person and then respond to it. This completes the communication circuit which promotes understanding.
- We usually are closest to and feel the most comfortable with people who listen well. There is a difference between being a good listener and just being polite when someone else is speaking and not really interested in what is being said.
- Be careful not to let emotions get out of hand in a conversation.
- Learning to communicate effectively requires being able to be sensitive to the other person.
- A good listener does not always think of a person's wealth or social status before he or she thinks that they can learn something from that person. It is being flexible enough that you find you can enjoy the conversation with an 8 year old child or the chairman of the board of a large corporation.
- Listening is a discipline that requires concentration and endurance.
- When a person is a good listener, he or she does not jump to any conclusions about the speaker.

CHAPTER 15

Proverbs 31:25
"She is a woman of strength and dignity, and has no fear of old age." LB

GROWING OLDER WITH GRACE

One of the things that all of us are aware of happening to us is that we are all growing older. Some of us do it gracefully, some of us do not. When we were 20 we thought that we would be young all of our lives, and then all of a sudden 20 or 30 more years have gone by. If the body and mind are taken care of, you can remain strong physically and mentally but it takes work. There may be a few more gray hairs and a few more wrinkles, but learning to accept these changes can give a more positive look on maturing. Fortunately there is a new attitude about older people now and what they can and cannot do, mostly what they can do.

GENERAL TIPS

- You need to spend some time playing and just enjoying life. It is great to be a great success but it is also good to give yourself permission to enjoy some leisure activities.
- A truly happy and glowing person is someone who is satisfied in all aspects of life.

- Having some very rewarding relationships adds to this satisfaction and fullness of living.
- Develop a method for coping with stress. You might try some breathing exercises, regular amounts of exercise, and listening to your favorite music.
- Trusting that there is a God that loves you and cares for you can give a serenity that nothing else can quite accomplish.
- Regular periods of prayer and watching our faith increase brings a real glow to our countenance.
- Develop a hobby that is pleasing to you and relaxing. Some hobbies cause more stress than they are worth.
- Stress is an aging factor and a drain on your body and mind.
- Beauty begins on the inside both physically and mentally.
- I guess our attitude has more to do with what we do with our age than anything. Some older people think that everyone owes them something just because they are old and they can talk and act the way. they want but if you want to be pleasant to be around and someone that people admire, then check your attitude toward yourself and your age.
- Aging has a lot to do with an upright posture, enthusiasm, and excited speech. I read where one noted voice teacher says that if you talk with energy, it will make you ageless.
- Even the fashions that we put on have a lot more to do with how we see ourselves and the shape we are in than it does with age.
- Aging is an inch by inch process so neglect of ourselves may not be noticeable at the moment but over a period of time, the wear and tear will build up and become increasingly noticeable.
- As we get older posture is extremely important. Be aware of how you walk, sit, and stand and make an effort to keep your body in alignment. To have a springy gait in our walk will take years off of a woman's age. Be sure that your calcium intake is not being depleted which can cause a hardship in getting around as we get older. Get a good checkup with your doctor.
- Keep your nails and hands looking younger by sticking to medium earthy or rose shades. Dark or bright polish draws attention to spots.
- It is important as we get older to stay committed, involved, and right in the mainstream of life.
- Having something to do that makes you feel as if you are making a contribution in this world is very important.
- Work helps keep the wrinkles out of the mind and boosts the spirit.
- Attitude is always the most important attribute whether you are 20 or 80.

HAIR

- One mistake that many older women still hang on to is their longer hair and deep red lipsticks which only add to ones age. It is important to stay with the times and make changes that will bring out our best features.

- Many people think that long hair is youthful but most hairdressers agree that is actually quite aging and pulls the face down and elongates our face. As we get older we need more of an uplift in hairdos.
- It is the look of the hair many times even more than the make up that is important for image impact at any age, and that is even more true as we get older.
- After forty it is best to keep the hair a little shorter, simple and not trendy..
- Updating your hairstyle can take years off of a face. Nothing can date a woman faster than yesterdays hairdo.

FASHION

- If you want to dress with more authority with out an older look wear finer quality and more sophisticated subtle lines and coloring. Wear subtle colors or if you look really smashing in a bright color like electric blue.
- The sophisticated prints and geometric prints are better than the large flowers.
- Pretty colors are one of the easiest ways to put together an attractive wardrobe because a closet full of dull safe solids can add years to your fashion touch.
- Add a healthy amount of lively colors and prints and it will give a much younger look.
- Add some softer fabrics in blouses and they give the younger look also. The men's tweeds or strict pinstripes give the oldest image. A younger look in a suit is the short jacket bloused or fitted to the waist or even a peplum jacket.
- A soft flare over the hip with the peplum gives a younger look because they are soft compared to the larger out of proportion jackets. The figure needs to be slim to wear this.

MAKE UP AND SKIN CARE TIPS

- Be aware of your facial expressions because bad habits such as a squint or a scowl can leave its mark on your skin. The collagen understructure weakens from the continual expression and a wrinkle gets etched into the skin.
- Smiling deepens the lines from outside the nostrils of the nose to the corners of the mouth, where as squinting will give crows feet a good start.
- If you are a worrier or a scowler, you will get vertical furrows between the brows or perhaps some horizontal lines on the forehead.
- Pursing your lips as you smoke or just as a habit when concentrating, causes vertical lines along the top lip.
- You should not try to be expressionless but try to keep your facial muscles relaxed when not used for a particular purpose.
- Long term ultraviolet light damage can causes wrinkling, leathery skin and broken capillaries. Since cellular repair decreases with age, the older you get the less efficient your skin is at repairing the damage.
- The more fair your skin, the thinner your skin and the earlier you will show signs of aging. Begin protecting your skin early in life and be aware that a tan will not be good for your skin at all. You will need the most protection on the thinnest and driest areas of your face such as your eyes, neck, and cheeks.

- One big factor in adding more wrinkles to the skin is cigarette smoking. Anytime you have something that affects your body in a negative way will also affect your skin negatively.
- It is never too late to turn some bad habits into good so start today
- Be sure that a sound skin care system has been established such as a good moisturizer for the face and all over the body.
- If you have a craggy eyelid, use creamy powder and put it on your finger and then apply to the lid.
- The twenty year old can wear make up or skip it altogether but by our thirties more make up is needed for a more defined look. In the forties the make up needs to be a bit softer and by fifty a woman knows her best qualities and what to accent and what to soften.
- A thicker eyebrow gives a more youthful look than the thin plucked line or penciled in brow. Fill in with a soft stroke of eye shadow for a natural look.
- As we get older, some of the beauty tips that we used a few years ago make not be the best for us now. We all change with age and therefore so should our makeup. Every beauty expert has their own opinions about what is best but you need to consider who you are and what is best for you using some of the techniques and tips that have proven to be best. Here are a few tips.
- Jet black eyeliners are more aging than a softer line, so use the softer charcoal pencil and smudge it in.
- Shaggy brows accent sagging lids and deep lines.
- Be sure and check your liner and brows to be sure they are the same thickness on both eyes.
- Brow powder is best and is less harsh than brow pencil.
- Frosted lip, eye or cheek colors accentuate wrinkles so it is best to switch to a lighter foundation and stick with more smokey shadow colors.
- The foundation should be just enough to even out your skin appearance and should closely match your complexion.
- Always blend foundation well around the edges so you do not have a neck line.
- The loose powder will help to minimize hard lines.
- Make up is a form of fashion and changes with the times so take the current ideas and adapt them to what is best for yourself.
- When we get older we not only lose color in our hair but we lose color in our face as well so the more mature woman needs to apply color as we get older.
- One of the most aging things is when a woman gets the incorrect color in a makeup base and then carries that color into her clothes selection. The reflections from the wrong color will reflect the negatives in the skin and cause sallowness and then wrinkles become more obvious.
- Older skin loses color as well as moisture so a foundation is important to even out the skin tone.

- Older eyes do not look their best in heavy makeup. Color on a craggy lid is not attractive and blue, green or turquoise are some of the most unbecoming colors. Stay with the soft muted shades and ones that will not accentuate the eye.
- As we age, it is best to stick to the subtle neutral shades.
- As we age, do not use the iridescent powder because it will exaggerate lines and wrinkles.
- The two most important things to keep skin from aging is cleaning the skin gently and protecting it adequately.
- If you want to avoid unwanted facial wrinkles then sleep on your back so you do not push wrinkles into your face.
- If you clench your teeth or tense up your face when under stress, you will show aging lines.
- If muscles continually contract, then they enlarge, stretching the skin that lies over them and stretched skin eventually sags and becomes wrinkled.
- The habit of frowning or scowling can etch wrinkles or lines into your skin.
- Catch yourself when you begin to tense up your face and consciously relax those right muscles.
- Reappraise your make up colors about every five years to check and see if they are still giving you the best look for your age.
- As the skin ages, the face becomes drier and more lined. This will make foundation sink into the skin and accentuate lines around the eyes and mouth. If this is a problem, choose subtle colors for eyes and lips to counteract grayness.
- There is no reason why at age 50 or over your skin should not be soft and supple and hair shining and healthy. Nevertheless, menopause does take its toll on the condition of the skin and hair as some of the hormones decrease. At this time a good facial scrub is important to ensure that the skin texture remains smooth and glowing. The skin is drier and more delicate so use only the mildest of scrubs.
- Rethink your skin care program and make up techniques every five years from about the age of 40. A skin that is drier and looks flaky may need a mild exfoliant once a week and a richer moisturizer at night. The throat and neck area tend to age rapidly so always start moisturizing from the collar bone up. Some neck exercises would be good also, such as opening your mouth and tightly pulling the bottom jaw up in a chewing motion.
- Cosmetics can subtract years from the face but they need to be applied more carefully in the older years. Layers of foundation and face powder can be very ageing because it will settle into the creases of the skin bringing out every line so use a lighter hand when making up.
- Apply a thin layer of moisturizing foundation with a damp sponge and cover with a soft translucent powder.
- Keep to the barest minimum around the eyes where wrinkles are easily emphasized.
- Choose a foundation that is close to your natural color which may be a little lighter than it was when you were younger.
- Keep the blush, lip, nail and eye colors neutral and soft. No blue eye shadows.

- Loading on makeup and accessories is fun and is done with the fashion looks but too much can be aging.
- Simplicity is better.
- Although the creamy lipsticks moisturize the lips, women who are older should wear the no smear lipsticks instead because creamy will tend to get into the wrinkles around the mouth accentuating them. Lip liners will help to eliminate this problem.
- Although you lose color in your hair as you get older, you also lose color in your skin.
- Lighter colors are less aging so instead of coloring your hair too dark, try having the lightest strands brightened a shade or two.
- When we get older it is best to soften the makeup colors, wear less hair spray, and use a nonglaring nail polish.
- If you go on a crash diet which many women do, you make the problem worse by losing muscle and the result is a sagging appearance.
- Too much make up is very aging. This doesn't mean that a woman is better off with no makeup at all. Nearly every woman needs to wear an under eye concealer and foundation which will smooth out the imperfections in the skin.
- Age and grey hair drain color from the skin.
- 95% of wrinkles that show up on your skin are caused by the sun.
- The darker the skin the more protection that you have from the suns rays so if you are very light skinned, always use a sun protectant.
- Spite some water on your face and then apply your moisturizer with a gentle patting motion. Finish getting dressed while this soaks into your face.
- You do not have to buy the most expensive moisturizer to get good results.
- It has been said over and over that sun will cause aging much quicker than if you take time to protect your face from the ultraviolet rays.
- Heredity also plays a part in aging so your parents faces provide a good visual look at how you will age. However, heredity is not necessarily bad for you because there are many new treatments and preventive measures today to help signs of aging.
- There are some women of forty that look thirty and vice a versa which may say that it has something to do with the way we take care of ourselves. It helps to have good genes but even if we do and do not take care of our skin, it will eventually catch up with us and heredity does little good.

EXERCISE

- When you begin an exercise program begin slowly and build up gradually. If you do not exercise in mid life then the joints will stiffen and your body will function less efficiently.
- The experts say that if you exercise at least four times a week, you can expect good results.
- Replacing fat with muscle through the proper diet and exercise program allows us to carry more weight.

- Exercise will very good for your skins because it increases circulation and promotes the delivery of oxygen and nutrients to the skin as well as removing wastes.
- Once again, proper diet nourishes the whole body including the skin.
- If you are losing weight, then do it slowly enough so that the skin does not get saggy and wrinkled. If you do it slowly, the skin can keep up with the fat volume loss.
- Take responsibility for your own health and make it a priority if you want to preserve your looks for the advancing years. As you get older you tend to lose muscle and gain fat and the result is a middle age spread. The key point then is to get a good form of exercise as a regular regime to build muscle.
- Start with regular exercise. Do not start an exercise program without some information and instruction on what is best for you.
- Get plenty of fresh air and sleep.
- Eat a balanced diet. A lot of women eat the same amounts and types of food in mid life as they did as teenagers and then do not understand why they no longer weigh the same. The problem is as we get older metabolism slows down so that the body burns fewer calories in its resting state so you need to eat about 100 fewer calories a day for each decade after 40.

SLEEP

- Sleep is important at any age, but if neglected over a long period of time it will really show up in the face.
- When you get over tired from not enough rest and sleep, circulation is diverted away from the face to major muscles and organs and drains the color from your skin. This is where you get an unhealthy looking pallor and make the dark under eye circles obvious.
- Relaxing is essential to beauty and getting enough sleep and rest are very good for wrinkles and give you a refreshed look.
- This may not be possible for most people, but a 15 minute rest in the morning and afternoon can be a great refresher. This is a rest period without visiting or interruptions.
- Sleep is important and everybody's sleep needs vary.
- If you have trouble getting to sleep, try this relaxing tip. Put on some soft music and add your favorite scented cologne or bubble bath to the tub. Put moisturizer all over your body before getting into the water. Then drink a glass of warm milk while soaking and soak 10 min.
- When you get out you will be ready for a good nights sleep.
- If you have a hard time going to sleep, try rising earlier in the morning and continue doing this until you are sleepy at your bedtime hour.
- Go to sleep when you are tired, not when its time to go to bed.
- If you feel wide awake, capitalize on having some extra time to do some things you want to do.
- Fresh air and gentle exercise are two good sleep inducers particularly if they ar done just before bedtime.

- Try getting up an hour earlier in the morning.
- Do not eat to much food just before bedtime.
- Some of the experts say that cheese, milk and yogurt are all good night foods.
- Milk is especially good as a nighttime food because it contains high levels of amino acids which seem to play a significant part in producing sleep.
- High carbohydrates before bedtime are not good.
- Do not take stimulants before bedtime such as alcohol, sugar, salt, coffee, tea, and cola drinks. These may act as a metabolism stimulant for up to 7 hours.
- Take a warm bath before you go to bed and it will soothe and relax you.
- Check your surroundings to be sure that you are comfortable in bed. You may tend to sleep better in other beds if the mattress is too hard or too soft.
- Check your background noise and see if that may be disturbing you and you are completely unaware of it.
- Sleep in a bedroom away from the street noises.
- Make sure that your windows are fitted more tightly.
- It is easier to fall asleep in a crowded room with all the windows shut because the amount of oxygen available is gradually being displaced by carbon dioxide.
- Take time to unwind before going to bed by listening to soft music, reading, or looking at something pleasant.
- Warm milk has soothing ingredients to help sleeplessness.
- Take a warm but not too hot bath not a shower.
- Be careful what you eat in the evening because some food such as chocolate, coffee, tea, etc. can be very stimulating.
- Learn to make priorities because you may have said yes when you should have said no to an activity that causes you undo stress and sleeplessness.
- Avoid activities that irritate you. You will be surprised when you take stock of your life how you can eliminate some irritations without causing any offense to someone.
- Do one thing at a time and follow through so that you do not have things worrying you that need to be done.
- If you have trouble getting to sleep, try this relaxing tip. Put on some soft music and add your favorite scented cologne or bubble bath to the tub. Put moisturizer all over your body before getting into the water. Then drink a glass of warm milk while soaking and soak 10 minutes. When you get out you will be ready for a good nights sleep.

CHAPTER 16

Phil. 3:14
"I press on toward the goal to win the prize for which God has called me heavenward in Christ Jesus." NIV

GOAL SETTING

All of us have things that we do not like to do and sometimes getting organized enough in our lives to get a fresh start in life or shaping up a plan for improving our image or our lives in general takes months or even years but if you do not start and set some goals no changes will ever take place.

- Decide in your mind what needs to be changed and set some goals on how to do get started. Decide in your mind what cannot be changed and accept it.
- Identify the problem whether it is extra weight you want to take off, finishing up college, or what may be a goal for you. Target your goal and then work out a plan to achieve your objectives.
- Head and heart goals are fine but if you really want to accomplish that goal, it will require planning and having it down on paper in some concrete way.
- Get rid of all the excuses made for not reaching goals such as too busy, too old, too tired or whatever it may be. Now move beyond those excuses and take the first step.
- Set some time limits for starting the goal and then finishing it. Reward yourself in the interim for small accomplishments and be sure that the goal you have set is a realistic one. Losing 20 pounds in I week is not a realistic goal or you are not going to be able to completely improve a relationship in a day.
- Surround yourself with positive supportive people who believe in you and improve your life.

- Assess where you are today. Take out a piece of paper and find a quiet corner and begin to think about the many aspects of your life. Take some time to write down the good qualities and write down the things that you can improve. Do not be too hard on yourself but be honest.
- Be honest with yourself on what excuses you use to keep from improving yourself in each area.
- Go through your lists and circle the things you could improve and put a check by the things that you need to learn to accept, such as if you think that you are too tall, that is something that you need to learn to accept and let it work in a positive way for you.
- Once you have identified some of your problem areas, then you need to analyze in greater depth those things that you really want to improve and what time and effort it will take.
- If you write down on paper such things that you want to improve about yourself mentally, physically, and spiritually, it will b easier for you to accomplish these goals when they are before you on paper.
- Once you have gained an understanding of your areas that you want to improve, its time to take action.
- Set up specific accomplishments. For instance if you want to lose weight, you need to come up with the exact number of pounds you need to lose to reach your goal and the time you need to do it in.
- If you want to improve your marriage, identify the areas that need changing. Begin to measure your progress by spending one evening a week alone with your spouse.
- Remember that goals are usually not reached over night so be realistic
- Set a target date that you want to realize some positive changes taking place.
- Get cheerleader people to help you over some of the humps like a good friend that will cheer you toward your goal.
- Lack of communication causes so many people to lose sight of a goal and give up on themselves, their marriages and sometimes just life. If you do not communicate, many unresolved things are harbored and ends up in negative responses and actions instead of positively pushing on toward your goal.
- Have your goals before you every day. This is why it is important to have them written down. Write them on a small card and put them in places in the house or work where they can be read often.
- Realize that just because you have committed yourself to a goal does not mean you may not lose some ground once in awhile. It happens to all of us from time to time but do not let a small set back abandon your goal altogether.
- Do not condemn yourself to failure for when you do this you are letting negative thinking reinforce your thoughts of failure.
- Plan something special for yourself when you reach your goal.
- Concentrate on the positive reward you will receive every time you are tempted to give up.

- Set intermediate goals if what you have set to accomplish will take more than a month. The rewards do not have to be expensive — perhaps something as simple as a rose set on your desk will lift your day.
- When you give yourself a reward it is saying that you believe in your ability to set a goal and achieve it.
- You need a clear picture of what you want to accomplish. That's why writing things down helps us to accomplish this.
- Write your one year goals first, then six month goals and then three month goals. You get a much more positive outlook in accomplishing what you want this way because something that we could never do for a month we could do for a week. Inch by inch.
- Goals are some specific end result that you want and activities are those things that you do to meet the goal.
- A goal has to be specific and concrete. Sometimes a goal is realizing that what you need to do is to simply enjoy what you already have.
- You may think that you are in the same place that you were yesterday but what you need to realize is that we will never again be where we were yesterday for we have moved into a fresh new day. Its what we do with it that really counts.
- Learning to set life goals gives you an identity.
- Many mid life crises come when you fool around all of your life with no specific goals set and then begin to realize there are not that many more years on this earth to so what you want to do.
- Everyone's goals are different and that is what makes you different. God makes no two flowers or snowflakes, or people exactly alike.
- Learn to control your days and what you accomplish in them instead of letting them control you.
- Jack LaLanne said something that I thought was very good. He said "you have twenty four hours every day to do what you want and you are the sum total of how you use those hours." He certainly is the visible proof of someone who set a goal and accomplished it.
- Most people do not think in terms of minutes, so they waste so many of them.
- Make a list of all your time leaks.
- Keep up to date two things — a notebook and a calendar. The calendar can stay at home and the notebook should be small enough to travel with you and this will help you organize your life.
- To take some stress out of your life and your daily goals, do things early and ahead of time. Do not be a last minute person for the stress level gets too high and the things you wanted to do are not done as efficiently.
- Keep going even when you have taken two steps backward.
- Determination, self control, and consistency are three things that are needed to reach goals. Maybe to have more self control over something like a temper could be one of the goals, then let the determination kick in and watch self control become a reality.
- Make your goals very specific.

- Goals will enable you to have control of your life and to take charge of your time and resources.

CHAPTER 17

Ecclesiastes 3:l
"There is a time for everything, and a season for every activity under heaven." NIV

TIME MANAGEMENT WILL TAKE SOME ORGANIZING

In this world where most everyone needs to work to earn a living, it takes more time management and organization to be able to handle all of the things that vie for our time.

A CALENDAR AND NOTEBOOK

- Get a big wall calendar and use a different color pen for every member of the family when making obligations, meetings, and other appointments. Then everyone can see what the other member of the family is doing and when.
- Keep a notebook handy with data. facts, and numbers that you use frequently and it will make it easier. Keep birthdays, addresses, clothes sizes, and anything else that your life requires you to remember.
- Make a daily to do list. Then put it in priority order and organizational order so that you are not running here and there and having to retract your steps.
- The secret is to use the note book and not let it sit in the drawer.

- Your small notebook organizer should include a calendar, daily, weekly and monthly appointments, an address section, telephone number section, household planning section, and any other divisions that would pertain to your life style.
- Keeping a calendar of appointments and things to do will keep you from overlapping responsibilities and can help you to remember important dates.
- Try organizing your handbag so that the small irritation of trying to find something in it is removed and your efficiency increased.
- Keep a notebook in your handbag that is organized into sections and is filled with things to get done or buy. sizes, etc. Then when you are out of your home, you will have the information handy and will not have to guess at purchases. If you will keep a notebook not only with you color key, sizes, etc., but you life goals, books you want to read, sizes of others, things to get done, then it will make life easier for you to remember and you will do less back tracking.
- A yearly calendar gives an all over view of the year, the monthly calendar can be glanced at for appointments that are not on the standard routine and the daily calendar gives your perspective for the day.
- Get yourself an organizer notebook or make one yourself with a small purse size binder and some blank tabs for labeling as well as a calendar.
- List on the tabs according to your life needs such as your daily appointments and duties from morning to evening.
- Many things we intended to get done whether we work outside the home or are a homemaker do not get done because we simply forgot to do them. This can be eliminated when things are written down.
- One of your sections could contain your calendar where you can look and get a quick view of what you need to do daily as well as for the month. It can be as simple a duty as getting a report written to sending a birthday card.
- One thing that I keep that has been valuable is a separate little book with blank pages which I can write on when I hear something that I want to remember either from someone or even on the radio. If it touches my heart I write it down so that I will not forget what was said or I might just write down my thoughts and feelings for that day. I call this my memory book.
- One of your sections should say miscellaneous where you can keep lists such as various phone numbers including emergency ones, your husbands social security number, clothes sizes of people you buy gifts for, or just anything that makes your life easier by not having to go home and look it up before accomplishing a task.
- Write down your every day activities that need to be accomplished because it is easier to remember what to do and gives you a feeling of accomplishment when you can cross things done off of a list.

GENERAL ORGANIZATION AND TIME MANAGEMENT TIPS

- Time management means to use your time wisely while organization is the way you can get everything done in the time that you have.

- To become more effective in plugging up time waster holes, begin to identify where your time goes by keeping a time diary for just a week and write down how much time you spend doing various tasks, as well as breaks and interruptions. This will probably give you some interesting discoveries.
- You might find that you waste time the same way during a specific time period each day. When you identify this, then you can plug up the hole.
- You might find that you are more productive at various time of the day. Do the most concentrated and hardest tasks at this time.
- You might discover that there are certain people that waste your time every day. The important thing is that you begin to see precisely how and where your time gets away from you.
- Do things ahead of time is one of the best tips for organization and time management.
- Keep things in your life handy and uncluttered.
- Think ahead. If your summer shoes need repairing, then get them done ahead of time so that they will be ready when you need them or if your bike needs fixed before spring do it before you need it the next hour. Get your lawn mower repaired in the winter so you do not have to wait to use it in the summer.
- Have a personal desk or place where you can keep the things that you use often to prevent having to look all over the house for an item such as a pen or paper clip.
- Buy all occasion cards in a box and stationery as well as a book of stamps so that you will not have to run to the store everytime that you want to send someone a greeting.
- Keep sharpened pencils, pens, paper clips, various notepads, a stapler, rubber bands and various other things that you find yourself using frequently in this desk area.
- Keep running around to a minimum and the efficiency level will get higher.
- Think ahead and this is one of the most effective defenses against anxiety and surprises in your daily routine. This will really simplify your life by not leaving things to the last minute.
- Try buying more than one item of something and it will save a lot of time. Do this not only in groceries but also items such as underwear, stockings, handkerchiefs, etc.
- Keep things on hand for emergency forgotten special days and it will add to your efficiency. An example would be birthday candles, etc.
- When things are on sale such as towels and you are already in town shopping, buy some items that would be good for weddings, showers, etc. and you will always have something on hand for an emergency or when you do not have time to shop.
- Keep a supply of wrapping paper, string, scotch tape and boxes handy to wrap gifts and it will make life easier when you need them.
- When you are cooking, fix extra portions and freeze them. This is good for dishes like lasagna and on that hurried evening, you can just pop it in the oven and put your feet up for a while.
- Plan your laundry time so that when the dryer is finished you will be there to take the clothes out and fold them and this will save refluffing the clothes or even ironing.
- Keep a jar of loose change handy at all times.

- Learn not to waste time, not only in the things that we do but in harboring anger and bitterness.
- Do not put off until later what you should be doing now. Procrastination is one of the greatest time wasters that there is and sometimes when we put it off, it may require more time later on.
- One time waster and energy expender is spending a lot of time on the telephone. Block most of your calls for one period of the day and it will help with telephone efficiency.
- Keep a drawer to clean out that is close or something else you can do while talking on the phone.
- Start eliminating unnecessary tasks. Many times we do them because we have always done them.
- Learn to include people in your world in things that you are doing by delegating some duties. In the long run this will make the person you ask feel good about the task as well as taking some pressure off of you.
- Worrying can sometimes immobilize people and is a real time waster. Most of the time, the thing we worry about never comes to pass. If you are worrying about something you have no control over, ask God to take the burden and take care of it and then leave it there.
- Disorganized people seem to work harder than organized people. They end up having to work extra hours just to get everything done and they end up tense.
- Disorganized people tend to become slaves to the clock. They work to beat the clock rather than making time work for them.
- Pick up as you go. Do not leave everything go and then pick up all that you have left for days at one time. Keep your world pleasant and uncluttered.
- People who get what they want out of life learn to eliminate clutter from their lives in order to concentrate on what is important.
- It has been shown that if you could save one hour each working day during a normal career, you could add the equivalent of six years to your career.
- It becomes a habit to save time so begin to break some bad habits and replace them with good ones until finally they become second nature to us.
- Keep things handy to be done while waiting for an appointment or if you are delayed some other way.
- They say that Americans do not read as much as they should so always keep a book handy in your handbag or car so that if you are caught in traffic or end up waiting in your car for something you can catch up on your reading.
- You manage your time and do not let the time manage you. Work by appointment. If you have a very busy schedule, if you will make out a list of things that need to be done by a certain time and then give yourself time limits on what needs to be done, you will be surprised how much you can accomplish.
- If you will pull all the details of a meeting that you have attended together and not leave things hanging in the air, it will leave one less thing to figure out later.

- One real time waster regarding meetings is a meeting that is unnecessary in the first place or a meeting that goes too long. It is important to start on time, stick to the business at hand and end the meeting on time.
- Keep on hand telephone numbers that you call frequently.
- Time management is important but so is relaxation and if you will learn to be better organized you will have more relaxation and recreation.
- If you start a task with the correct attitude, it will not seem as arduous and will get finished faster.
- If you have a list of things that need to be done, start with the one that you dislike the most and go to the most pleasant ones as you progress and get more tired.
- Take short breaks to refresh yourself and takes some deep breaths.
- If you put off what you need to do, worrying about what you have to do robs you of energy and pretty soon you are too tired to do the task.
- Think of a big job in small accomplishments. Whenever I have a large job to do such as a closet, I think of doing just a certain amount and then a little more etc, until it is finally done. Inch by inch is much easier than thinking of how big it is.
- Do not start a big job late in the day or when you are tired or when you will not be able to finish it.
- Sometimes we just have to say that tomorrow is another day.
- Be very aware of interruptions and intrusions because they can really sap your energy. Do not let people control you such as with the telephone but set some limits. However, to me people are much more important than things and the intrusion should certainly be considered regarding the need of the individual.
- If your life requires a good deal of telephone time, get yourself a long cord installed so you can move about freely to do other things.
- Make your bathroom an easy place to clean by keeping out of the way a small plastic wastebasket with all the brushes, sponges, and cleaners needed to clean the room.
- A lot of energy is expended just gathering tools to do a task. Sometimes it takes twice as long to gather up things than to do the job itself.
- It is important to give yourself fingertip control such as being able to find things easily and keeping items such as scissors, sewing items or whatever within an arms reach.
- The principle that is important in organization is that there is a time and place for everything.
- Don't forget to give yourself a time slot for your wants tos as well as the things you must do.
- The more that you are organized the less anxiety you will feel.
- If you are not getting things done as you would like, take a good look at your schedule and see if you are doing too much. If you are, set some priorities.
- A big time waster is not only doing the wrong things, but doing things the wrong way.
- Some people have a problem saying no and need to learn to do that. If you will think that in order to say yes to someone, you will need to say no to someone else. Our families must have priority in our lives because I think that is the reason there are so

many conflicts in the world today, The breakdown of the family as a priority in the lives of its individuals is no longer important.

- If you have promised to do something with your family for the night and another intrusion vies for your time, give first priority to your family and say no to the other.
- Relaxation is not wasted time. All of us need it and need some time for ourselves so plan it into your schedule.
- Plug up the holes that cause us to lose time like sand slipping through our fingers.
- Combine activities like doing your exercises while watching TV. or using the exercise bike while catching up on your reading.
- If you have a lot of errands to be done and no time, try hiring a teenager to pick up some of the slack and deliver some things to your home that could save you some precious time.
- When going to the grocery store, go with a list so that you do not forget and have to run back and go at a time when there are fewer lines.
- Sometimes we attempt to do something that would take a professional only minutes to do like our tax preparation. Let professionals do some real time consuming things.
- Don't go through life without a plan. So plan tomorrow by setting out the clothes you are going to wear.
- If you are going on a trip, make a packing list a week in advance to allow for dry cleaning, etc. This will take a lot of stress out of last minute things that pop up.
- If you wait for perfect conditions to do things then you will never get anything done because there are seldom perfect conditions.
- Divide the large tasks into several small ones and then they will not seem so overwhelming.
- It is important to plan your days and then stick to the plan. One of the things that helps you stick to what you have outlined is making lists.
- Set deadlines for getting things done and tell someone else your deadline.
- If you admit that you are procrastinating you will be half way there to stop.
- Reward yourself for finishing a job and carrying it through.
- If you go to a seminar on time management or read a book on how to do something and do not put it into practice, it is like not knowing it at all. To just hear or read something, and not act on it is in itself a waste of time.
- Plans should always be able to be revised. Don't pursue a plan to the bitter end if you can see that some revision needs to be done.
- If your schedule is continually interrupted, learn to reschedule your day. Leave enough time to do the things that you have scheduled so that those interruptions do not throw you clear off schedule.
- Set up a good filing system for bills, receipts, recipes, etc. The purpose of a filing system should be to retrieve something not to store it.
- Eliminate frustration by realizing that there is no way that you can do everything you would like to do absolutely perfectly all the time all by yourself exactly when you planned to do it.

- One of the greatest times wasters is not being able to find something when we want it so create places for things.
- Keep things separated in their own place. It is frustrating to try and find something when yarn, marbles, and coupons are mixed together.
- If you will create a place for everything, you will find that your world will become less complicated and frustrating. This may take some time to do but do it inch by inch.
- Don't flip the TV on and then spend the whole evening watching shows you never intended to watch and actually did not even enjoy them. This is a real time waster so get control of your time and use it so that you are following your schedule not someone else's.
- When you schedule your time, think of it in the same way that you budget your money. Invest some in the future and enjoy the present.
- It is the unscheduled people that never have enough time to get everything done and relax.
- Schedule activities that require a greater concentration from you during your peak production times. All of us have times of day we work better. Some people are morning people some are evening.
- When you begin to organize, begin with yourself first and then move into other areas of your life such as job and home.
- You need to set goals for what you want to accomplish in a specific time period. It is one thing to schedule an hour to work on a project but quite another to set specific goals as to what you want to accomplish in that hour. It is results that count not just staying busy.
- One of the greatest time wasters is procrastination. Just jump in and get it done and it is amazing what a boost this can be to your day and also a great burden is lifted when a task you really did not want to do is done.
- You can give yourself 10 or 15 minutes more sleep on weekday mornings by planning your weeks wardrobe in a half an hour on a Saturday.
- Write down and put together the clothes in your closet you plan to wear for the week including shoes, hosiery, jewelry. Include in your plan after work dates, important meetings and more casual days.
- Plan something special that you want to do when a particular task you have been dreading and avoiding is done. Then when it is done you have two things to be happy about, the task is done and the reward you gave yourself.
- If you find you cannot keep things neat no matter how hard you try, do not just assume that you are poorly organized — Maybe you have a flawed environment that can be changed to be more efficient and pleasant.
- Our surroundings can sap our energy also. Do you have a comfortable bed, cluttered areas that sap energy or uncomfortable areas in which you work like your kitchen.
- One energy waster is to be unorganized enough so that everytime that you want to do something or wear something, many minutes of energy is wasted trying to find that something that you need.

KITCHEN ORGANIZATION

- When you begin to organize your cupboards, begin with the one closest to the sink and methodically go around the kitchen.
- Take everything out, clean, and throw out or give away anything that is not used frequently.
- Pile the seldom used items in a kitchen overflow box.
- When you put things back, put the most used items in the front and seldom used ones in the back or on the highest shelves.
- Odd items such as vases and odd dishes should be boxed and stored to reduce kitchen clutter.
- Eliminate clutter in your utensil drawer by putting frequently used items such as wooden spoons, ladles, whisks, spatulas, and rubber scrapers into a crock or ceramic pot.
- Keep all of your knives sharpened so that they are ready to use.
- Use a plastic divider usually used for flatware in the junk drawer to organize tacks, nails, batteries, glue, etc.
- Keep your pantry just for food. No papers items, books, or toys. Label shelves according to foods such as soups, fruits, vegetables, cereals, etc. Keep the baking section separate with flour, sugar, baking soda and mixes. Keep the packaged items such as dressing mixes, etc. in a large jar or a small box to keep from getting scattered.
- Keep everything that you can from tea bags, to flour, crackers, noodles, coffee, etc. in jars.
- Store appliances that work together on the same shelf such as mixing bowls, mixers and measuring cups.
- Keep all pans together and if you have enough room you can line the shelf with paper and draw an outline of the pan and then store it in its designated place.
- Being able to find things is one of the best organizational tools I know of.
- Lazy Susans are helpful in the refrigerator to hold items such as sour cream, cottage cheese, jellies, mustard etc. Then you can just turn it around to get the item.

CHAPTER 18

I. Corinthians 6:20
"... therefore honor God with your body."
NIV

WET WATER TIPS — SWIM SUITS AND BATHS

On a hot day, nothing beats a dip in a cool pool but many women just will not put on a swim suit because of a self consciousness of their figure. There are some things that can be done to look your best in a swim suit.

SWIM SUITS

- Lines are very deceiving so use them to achieve a certain look so slim areas with vertical lines and widen areas with horizontal lines.
- When looking for a suit, be sure that it is sewn correctly. For instance, the neckline should have no gaps and if the back is low, it should hug the body.
- The swim suit straps should leave the shoulder blades free to move for swimming but not so loose that they fall down.
- Look for double or reinforced stitching at the straps, sides, back, and legs.
- The fabric should be a durable one. Nylon suits last longer and cost less, however, they tend to leave gaps after awhile.

IF YOU ARE HEAVIER:

- If you are heavier than you wish, then do not choose a material that is too shiny or too bright a color.
- Do not choose large flowers or horizontal lines if you are heavier.
- If you have added pounds, choose a one piece suit in a descending darker and duller finish color.
- Also, the V neckline cut would be the most flattering to create a vertical line and more height and slimness.
- Do not choose a bold pattern.
- Do not choose gathered skirts over the hipline because it will add extra bulk and inches.

NO FIGURE PROBLEM, BUT SHORT LEGS.

- A high cut leg suit would add length to the bottom half of your figure.
- Do not choose suits that have a skirt that cuts across the top part of your legs.
- Choose vertical striping to add leg length.

IF YOU FEEL YOU ARE TOO SKINNY.

- Add some width with horizontal stripes.
- Choose a fabric that has more bulk than the nylon suit.
- Choose a suit with prints and more design than most people can wear.
- Bikini suits are not good if you are too bony.
- Suits with skirts that add some bulk and width are good.
- Square necklines or the soft boat necklines would be good as well as the rounded neckline.
- Two tone striping is good.
- The soft flow diagonal lines are good also.
- Wear the brighter more ascending color and shiny fabrics.

THICK WAIST, TOO MUCH HIP, AND TUMMY BULGE.

- Choose a blouson top that softly drapes over the waistline and top of hip.
- Avoid ruffles, lace or any detail around the waist or hipline that would draw attention to that area.
- Soft diagonal shirring over waist and tummy area can help hide not only the waist but the tummy bulge.
- Soft skirting can help hide tummy bulges.
- White increases size and adds inches.
- Keep a beach bag handy so that you can have everything you need such as suntan lotions, towels, etc.

THE BATH

- If you have always been the no nonsense type of person who hurries up and takes a shower, you owe it to yourself to experience the tranquil pleasures of a bath. Health spas have long relied on the magic of water mixed with herbs, mud and the essential oils of plants or mineral salts to smooth skin, refine pores, relax tense muscles, and help our bodies feel rejuvenated.
- Most people take baths that are too hot. Frequent hot bathing can have a loosening effect on muscles and skin and can cause the skin to age.
- The temperature of a bath should be a warm 85 to 95 degrees.
- For a more stimulating bath, make it cool and a tepid bath before bedtime will help you sleep.
- Many European hydrotherapists use water as a healing agent from minor colds to pneumonia.
- Take time in your bath and light a few candle around the room to create a relaxing atmosphere.
- Put some of your favorite scent into the tub and let it make the air fragrant.
- A dry rough textured loofah sponge that you soften by wetting and rub it against the skin to slough off dead cells and increase circulation could be a great beauty aid.
- This is especially helpful for that dry skin on your heels when you wear opened toed shoes.
- A massage just before you get into the bath is good for very dry skin.
- Put a little baby oil into the bath with a few drops of your favorite cologne or perfume and the scent will cling to your body.
- Splash water onto your face and let it sit and soak in while you bathe.
- If you take baths, take a cool bath for 10 minutes but no longer and this will help you get a refreshing start.
- The cool water stimulates circulation. Hot water is not good for you because it dries and ages the skin and may even injure delicate capillaries and veins if it is too hot.
- Hot water can also weaken you and make you feel tired.
- If you have a hard time waking up in the morning, shower with warm water and slowly turn the water down to a cooler temperature. Breathe deeply in the shower as you let your whole body relax by dangling your arms and head. Let the shower beat on the nape of your neck, shoulders and back which are the key tension spots.

CHAPTER 19

Hebrews 13:2
"Do not forget to entertain strangers, for by so doing some people have entertained angels without knowing it." NIV

DON'T BE AFRAID TO ENTERTAIN

One of the great privileges of life is to have people into your home and enjoy great fellowship with them. It is important to put away some pride when we entertain and seek to serve them and make them feel like they are the most special people while they are in our homes. Many people can't seem to ask someone to their house for many reasons. They do not think that their home is either nice enough or clean enough. People just want your friendship and your company so put away some pride and entertain with a servant's heart.

- The number one purpose when we have guests into our home is to make them feel at ease. The smile that we give them and the warmth of a hug all give off this message.
- The purpose of having people in is to fellowship with them and put them at ease. People need to be shown that they are special to us and that we are glad to be with them.

- When you are invited for dinner, do not arrive early because those last few minutes may be just what the hostess needs to pull things together. Do not be late however.
- The conversation should also put people at ease so be considerate in what is talked about and be a good listener.
- It is always pleasant if you are having dinner, that a nice table setting can be used with a table cloth and an attractive centerpiece.
- Centerpieces might include flowers, fruit, some nice candles or a combination.
- If you do not have room for this type of setting, then improvise but don't stop inviting people just because you don't think you can do anything fancy. Some of the nicest entertainment is done buffet style.
- It is nice to have something esthetically pleasant to set a mood. like candles, flowers or the smell of potpourri.
- Etiquette may have been misunderstood because everyone thinks it involves rigid rules or impossible guidelines but it really means simply being kind to each other.
- Do not cook something exotic or special that you have never prepared before. Fix something you have done many times before.
- Plan a menu that will lend itself to being prepared ahead of time.
- Always serve your guests first and watch for refills so they do not sit without water or something that would make the meal more enjoyable.
- If you are kind and gracious, you will automatically be practicing the rules of etiquette.
- If you serve something that was highly successful, then write it down and why it worked so well so that you can repeat it the next time. It might be good to write who you served it to also so you do not repeat what you served them the next time.
- Set a mood for your dinner party because when you create an environment that makes you happy, it will create a happy atmosphere for your guests.
- Be organized and get things done ahead of time so that the joy of the occasion is not marred by stress and anxiety or pressure.
- Learn to be flexible.
- Use shortcuts as much as possible such as a dish that you can prepare days or even weeks ahead of time.
- Get your spouse involved in the planning or plan a party with a friend and share responsibilities.
- Be flexible in your decorating ideas. You do not need a lace tablecloth and crystal glasses to set a wonderful table.
- Candles are especially effective for a nighttime party. It is fun to use a few or put them in groups and use interesting candle holders such as cored apples etc.
- Some people get so involved in the preparation of food that they forget the purpose of the party is to be with their friends.
- The food should help the guests enjoy themselves but it should not be the most important ingredient of the party.
- Do not wait to have people in until your house is perfect because you will be missing some memorable times if you do.

- Always write a written thank you note to the host and hostess for the wonderful dinner party even though you have said thank you in person. It is always appropriate to send a thank you note anytime someone does something nice for you and of course for gifts.
- If you do not feel up to have a large dinner party, then start small with a few friends for dessert.
- When you have a party of any kind, forget yourself and concentrate on others then you will feel more relaxed and will enjoy yourself.

A FEW SIMPLE ETIQUETTE RULES

- Get yourself acquainted with some of the simple rules of etiquette because it is when you do not know what to say or do that the evening becomes a burden. Here are a few simple rules.
- Do not put your napkin on your lap until grace has been said or the hostess starts the dinner.. In a restaurant, do not take the napkin until the order has been given.
- The man's napkin goes over one knee.
- Do not shake a napkin out full but keep it folded in half. The exception would be a small luncheon napkin which you can open completely.
- Use utensils from the outside in.
- Do not cut your meat into many small pieces but cut one piece at a time and eat.
- Scoop soup from front to back.
- Use your napkin to blot lipstick so there are not lipstick marks on the glass. Do not drink until the mouth is empty so that particles of food do not get into the water.
- When eating a roll, tear and do not cut. Break off a bite size piece, butter and eat.
- Do not stab the food but scoop utensil under food and eat. The exception is lettuce which can be stabbed with the fork and eaten.
- Bread can be used as a pusher but not the finger.
- Do not chew with your mouth open.
- Never put a used utensil back on the table. Keep it on the plate and when you are finished eating the utensils should be placed at 12 or 4 o'clock on the plate to indicate such.
- Do not pick your teeth at the table. If you must get something out of your tooth, go to the bathroom to remove it.
- If you must leave the table before the meal is finished to answer the phone, leave the napkin on the chair.
- Do not fold a used napkin up nicely but place it as a used napkin to the side of the plate when the meal is finished.
- To remember how to remove plates and serve, think R for remove from the right, and so therefore you would serve from the left.
- You have heard all your life not to put your elbows on the table but it gives a warmer feeling if one arm rests on the table and you lean a little forward to visit with others. Do not put both elbows on top of the table and rest your head in your hands.

- It would be good to purchase an etiquette book to get a more indepth look at proper etiquette. If you do not know the rule for something, just remember that common sense should come into play and if you use that with some thoughtfulness you will rarely ever be guilty of bad manners.
- Develop all areas of beauty from the inside out, physical and mental so that you can be a person that people love to be around and have into their home.
- Manners are ways of behaving with polite standards but etiquette is a set of rules set up for proper social behavior and developed with the thoughtfulness for the other person in mind.
- Gum chewing is never proper in social situations. It is strictly for casual activity and if it cannot be done with out looking like a cow chewing a cud, don't do it.

BUSINESS PHONE ETIQUETTE:

- Be aware of how you answer the phone. It can make a lasting impression for an office. The telephone company suggests that you smile when you answer the phone because the voice will come across differently when smiling than when frowning.
- Being warm and cordial can make or break someone's day and may also determine if they are going to do business with you or not.
- Talk with a lower voice and pronounce the words clearly.
- Absolutely no gum chewing over the phone.
- Always identify yourself by your name and your business when answering the phone.
- Whenever a message is left call back promptly.
- Do not leave someone hanging on a phone call like their time is not valuable. I have heard from others that this makes them more angry at a business than anything.
- If you are conducting a business from your home, be sure that there is not yelling in the background such as young children and never let a small child answer the phone and proceed to say who is this?
- It has been recommended that you get an answering machine if you are hard to get a hold of.
- Proverbs says like apples of gold in a setting of silver is a word spoken in the right circumstances.

CHAPTER 20

Judges 18:6
"Go in peace. Your journey has the Lord's approval." NIV

TRAVELING CAN BE FUN: PACKING FOR THE TRIP

If you are about to embark on a trip or vacation, it is a good idea to give some forethought to your needs and be prepared.

- Choose a hairstyle that is easy for you to manage on the trip so that you do not have to wear rollers etc.
- This is the age when men and women are traveling more and more and sometimes deciding what to pack can really becomes a hassle.
- Get organized about a week before your trip and check on the weather in regards to where you are going.
- Make a packing list and keep it parred down.
- A few days before you are to leave separate your traveling clothes in the closet and each day try to eliminate a few pieces.
- The last day eliminate everything that you absolutely do not need. Many times the things we chose the first day can now be easily eliminated.
- Keep all of the basic pieces in one color scheme such as black and white or various shades of blue. Then choose brighter accessories to perk them up. Keep it simple.
- Use your layering techniques to be able to go from daytime into the evening without a complete change.

- If one piece you have packed does not go with at least three other items, leave it behind.
- Remember what you wear on the plane should be included in your coordinated pieces.
- Choose fabrics that are lightweight and do not wrinkle easily.
- A lightweight gabardine is a good fabric because it can be worn in all seasons.
- Take some wash and wear items that are easy for you to drip and dry.
- If you will bring a lot of accessories such as belts, scarves, and jewelry, you can create a multitude of looks.
- Do not take expensive pieces with you that could be lost or stolen.
- Take shoes that are easy to walk in and one pair of dressier shoes. If you decide to take your boots, then wear them to save space.
- When packing, get together a "be ready for anything" kit.
- Put your makeup in a special bag so that you do not need to worry that something important is left behind. You can do this as you get ready in the morning as you use each thing and then nothing will be left behind.
- Pack a few things for emergencies and unexpected situations such as a purse sized tissue, wash up towelettes, rubber bands, shower cap, aspirins, and sun tan lotions. Purchase the smallest size possible of these items and be sure to put them into unbreakable containers.
- Check the long range weather forecast for the area you will be going to visit.
- Make a list of all the activities that you will be doing such as swimming, dinner parties, meetings, etc. and be sure to include the forecast changes in weather.
- Do not take anything on a trip that you have never worn. A trip is not the place to break anything in.
- Always try something on that you have not worn for awhile and check for split seams, a hem that is out, or perhaps a stain.
- Never break new shoes in on a trip.
- Hang the things that you plan to take in the same place. It would be good to have some kind of rack or lay the clothes out on your bed so that you can get an overall picture and make sure everything works together. This will also help to keep from forgetting essentials or taking duplicates.
- Put the outfits together with belts, shoes, and accessories.
- Be organized on paper and make a list of the days that you will be gone and what you plan to wear and where you are going to wear it for each day.
- Check to see what combinations you can make so that you do not have to take as many clothes.
- Try to stay within your basic and neutrals in color and add one major color. If you do this you will need fewer accessories and even make up, as well as nail polish, etc.
- Buy some pretty plastic lined cotton bags for your cosmetics and one for your medicines and vitamins.

- Cut down on your last minute rush by restocking these little bags as soon as you return home with such essentials as small shampoo, toothpaste, extra toothbrush, laundry soap and other little extras that you may need.
- Start packing a few days before you are going to leave. Do not leave it to the last minute.
- Keep your bags open in your bedroom so whenever you think of something you need, you can stop and pack it.
- If you wear glasses, take along an extra pair and also a copy of your prescription for eyeglasses.
- Always take along prescriptions for medicines in case you need them. If you are traveling abroad, the customs officials may question drugs that you have packed or a refill in a strange city may be hard to get.
- Bring a sewing kit and safety pins.
- Take garments that do not wrinkle and will hang out when you get to your destination. Many times if you will hang them in the bathroom during your shower, the steam will take the wrinkles out.
- Take your most comfortable shoes, You will need a good pair of walking shoes for day and a pair of sandals for night.
- Take mix and match pieces. This is where knowing your color key comes in handy because everything that you generally put together not only fits in with your fashion but also coordinates in color.
- Pick a weekend color theme and build your wardrobe around it. Take interesting accessories and you will not have to take as many clothes.
- Many times you can just change the jewelry on an outfit and change it from day to evening. Add a pair of evening shoes and you are set to go.
- When you pack, zip, button and belt a garment before you pack it and it will lay flatter and get less wrinkles.
- Match the leg seams of the trousers and then fold them in half.
- Try to weave your clothes together so that they are snug in the suit case and then they will not shift as much and there will be less wrinkling.
- Place all heavy items like your hair dryer, cosmetic kit, jewelry roll or shoes on the bottom of the suitcase opposite the handle so that when you lift the suitcase the heavy items do not drag the clothes with them as they fall to the bottom anyway.
- You can save some room if you will roll some of your items like lingerie, T shirts, sweaters and knits and fit them snugly along the suitcase front.
- Stuff small items like belts and socks into shoes.
- If you will pack one complete outfit together you can unpack without disturbing the other pieces.
- Use the plastic bags to stuff sleeves and roll small items of clothing.
- Stash a collapsible bag or foldable water proof nylon bag into your suitcase so that you will have something to put your souvenirs in.

- Waste paper basket liners are great for packing sweaters and blouses, shoes, and use the dry cleaner bags to slide over larger pieces of clothing before folding. Plastic hold air and helps to cut down on creases.
- Use stockings and small items such as scarves to stuff shoulders of jackets and blouses.
- Fold crushable items like silk over cushions of sweaters.
- Pack skirts and dresses inside out so that the creases will be inverted and not show as much.
- Put pants, skirts, blouses and dresses on a thin hanger and each in a plastic cleaning bag. Then fold them into thirds and when you get to your destination you can just pull out the hanger, shake the clothes out and hang up.
- Sometimes hanging an item of clothing on a hanger over the bathtub and running hot water to make steam will get the wrinkles out.
- Pack last what you will use first.
- Make a list of everything that you pack and keep it with you so that if you lose anything you will have an easier time making a claim.
- Safety pins come in handy for hanging skirts and slacks.
- It is important to have the right tool such as the right bags and suitcases when you travel.
- When packing consider where you are going and cut everything down to a minimum.
- Hard edged suitcases make them easier to pack as they hold their shape but the soft top and bottom ones allow for expansion. Make sure when you purchase that they are tough.
- In order to handle your own baggage easier, pack in two smaller suitcases you can carry yourself rather than one large one.
- If you travel a lot, get yourself one of the portable luggage dollies or get the suitcases with the wheels and pull handle. Test to see that they pull easily.
- Use some personalized identification markings on your baggage that can be easily seen so that they do not get picked up by someone else who has similar luggage. Some bright colored tape or yarn around the handles is easily recognized.
- Do not use your name and address as an ID mark. Put your name and business address on the concealed flap or keep it inside the bag. There are sometimes people called spotters at airports who love to find names and addresses of people out of town and it gives them time to go a clean out ones apartment or home.
- Use some canvas safety belts around your luggage for safety to prevent them from coming open.
- The most efficient way to travel if you can is with carry on pieces only. Take a canvas under the seat duffel, a shoulder strap bag, and a garment bag with handles so you can fold and carry easily.
- Carry your medications, essential cosmetics in your handbag or tote that you carry with you so that you will have them with you should your luggage end up in Hong Kong and you in Los Angeles.
- Cottons and cotton blends pack well and are relatively fuss free.

- A black or navy basic dress would be good to take so you can wear it very simple in the daytime and with some elegant jewelry and heels at night.
- It is a good idea to pack a light weight nylon rain coat.
- Avoid looking too bare in the cities.
- To keep yourself feeling and looking fresh and comfortable, plan to hand wash your lingerie and clothes.
- Don't pack everything you just love to wear just in case because chances are that most of it will have to be lugged back home unworn.
- A robe is very bulky so do not pack it unless long cozy evenings are planned.
- When you are traveling, if you will slip your shoes into some old cotton socks they will not dirty up your other clothes or your suitcase.
- Planning is the key word.

PACKING A GARMENT BAG

- Learn to layer four or five garments on a single sturdy hanger.
- Fold one or two pairs of trousers over the garment bar and then put skirts flat over pants, then a dress folded lengthwise down the middle.
- On another hanger, layer blouses, four to a hanger, button the top button of each and stuff tissue paper in the sleeves.
- Jackets or coats go onto a hanger over everything else.
- Sweaters like pants are put over the hanger bars. This will give you maximum amount of clothing in a bag.

CHAPTER 21

Isaiah 62:5
"... as a bridegroom rejoices over his bride so will your God rejoice over you." NIV

LOOK GOOD AT YOUR WEDDING

WEDDING CLOTHES TIPS

Now that you have set the big date, it is time to start thinking about what you will wear when you walk down the aisle. It is important to look your very best on your wedding day and choose a dress that will emphasize your better figure features.

- If you are short and slender, choose a simple design line that will draw the eye upward and give you an illusion of height. Choose a long tapered sleeve or a single ruffle on the sleeve. Too much clutter will shorten you. A lightweight fabric would be best.
- If you are short and not slender, choose the higher neckline, a long tapered sleeve, a fabric that is not bulky, delicate to medium trim, and do not choose a shiny fabric.
- If you are tall and slender, you can use textured fabrics, trim and appliques that go around the body such as ruffles, and full sleeves. Softness and fullness would be good but when you are tall and slim, you can wear what will show off a model figure. An exception might be the empire line which would add more height.
- If you are tall and not so slender, stay away from short puffy sleeves and heavy trims. Use the vertical lines rather than the horizontal and do not choose a shiny fabric.

- Some of the traditional fabrics are satins, taffeta, crepe, or brocade, as well as lace and sheer overlays.
- A romantic fabric that is less traditional is the pique, organza, eyelet or the semisheer handkerchief linen.
- When choosing fabrics remember that crisp fabrics generally create a sculptured shape and the soft fabrics create a fluid line.
- When you handle a wedding gown, be sure that the area and your hands are clean.
- Be sure that your nail polish is dry. A bottle of seltzer may be used for emergency stains and a can of hairspray for any lipstick that may get on the gown. Be sure that you try it on an inconspicuous area that does not show before you use it.
- When you choose a wedding gown, keep in mind that people will be seeing you both from front and back so consider what is flattering from both ways. If you have a dierrere problem you will not want to add to it with a bustle of some sort. Also consider the neckline and bodice both front and back to emphasize your best features.

CHAPTER 22

Proverbs 31:30
"Charm is deceptive, and beauty is fleeting — but a woman who fears the Lord is to be praised." NIV

PERSONALITY PLUS: PERSONALITY ATTITUDES, POSITIVE AND NEGATIVE

Our image is reflected every day in our attitudes toward our work and toward others.

Many times people do not have a positive image because they are always fretting about what was or what might be. Since one cannot change the past and the future continues to march on, we might as well live as fully as possible in the here and now.

- Begin to look at yourself in a positive way, bringing forward your good points and positive features. In other words, love yourself. You will never be completely happy until you do.
- Our inner attitudes are extremely important because attitudes can make us appear either beautiful or unattractive to others and certainly it affects our daily living.
- Negativism can really dampen the spirits of those around you as well as make you less likeable.

- Be aware that you have the ability to make or break someone's day by your attitude towards them with a simple smile or a cruel word. By the way, this includes our families.
- One of the qualities right at the top of affecting lives in a positive way is enthusiasm. It is contagious and makes a person appear to be in love with life which in turn gives us a new perspective that maybe life isn't so bad after all.
- Constantly feed positive thoughts into your mind and you will feed positive thoughts into your emotions which in turn will produce positive actions.
- Read positive books and biographies of people who have succeeded.
- Make some friendships and cultivate relationships with positive people that will add to your live instead of subtracting from it.
- Keep a diary of all your achievements and list everything that you feel you have done well. When you do this, you will come to realize how much you are reaching your goal.
- All of us do things that we should not do and regret them. If you have, then go out of your way to set it right, then forget it. Easy to say but hard to do but necessary if our energies are to be expended on the positive and improve ourselves mentally and physically.
- We have many blessings we overlook when we begin counting so take time to meditate on the good things in your life.
- A sour attitude about life and a critical spirit does not take long to lose beauty both inwardly and outwardly.
- Sometimes we recognize that our attitude is bad, but we feel too defeated to do anything about it but nurse our hurts. However, this is when you begin to put some of the tips into play and talk to yourself about being pleasant even if when we don't feel it. Soon you will feel better.

WORRY, FEAR AND ANGER

- One of the top psychologists has his patients that worry a lot keep a worry notebook. When they find themselves worrying about past present or future, they are to write their concerns in the notebook and appoint a time to fret about them later. Often the problems do not seem as big later.
- Many people lose their positive self image because of fear.
- Fears can cause us to walk into a room and lose our smile because we are afraid of the roomful of people. It is easy then to flatten yourself against a wall all evening and stay there.
- Perhaps you have always wanted to do something that would require a bit of faith such as asking for a promotion or running for an office. Fear steps in a says what if I fail? It is easier to sit back and feel negative and unattractive than to risk defeat.
- Some of the greatest lesson ever learned come from having to pick ourselves up and step out and do something that requires stretching beyond our comfort zones.
- It is far better to step out and improve ourselves than continue in fear of failure and never try at all.

- Worry saps energy so have a firm determination not to waste time and emotion on what cannot be changed. Doctors tell us that much loss of energy is from psychological factors rather than physical.
- Guilt feelings and self pity are some great energy enemies.
- Don't give in to anger because that takes a lot of energy and most of the time it is hard on our bodies.
- It takes longer to recover from anger than to get angry.

GENERAL TIPS

- A good image to portray is someone with a good sense of humor. When you begin to look at the craziness of everyday situations, it can make things not look as dismal.
- There seems to be a direct connection between physical activity and personal well being and being content.
- There are some studies that show that exercise can increase self esteem, relieve anxiety, help stress and elevate your mood.
- There is a certain level of exercise that keeps people happy and this varies with age and from person to person.
- People who lack meaning in their lives tend to be less happy with almost every aspect of their lives. This is why one person can be devastated by something in their lives and another with the same problem is able to rise above it.
- You need to develop a belief system in yourself to help you get through life and be everything that God created you to be. As one of the noted psychologists said, to believe in yourself will allow you to recognize your own self worth, to have an intelligent opinion, and to maintain your own identity.
- Try to see yourself as God looks at you instead of how you think people see you. God sees you as someone that is precious and important on this earth to carry out whatever plan he has for you. Seek God's plan and will for you and you will begin to see yourself as someone worthy and loved.
- Surveys show that those who are happy with their work are happy in general. Most people do not work extra hard just for the money.
- It is important to feel a sense of accomplishment in your work and it just plain makes you feel good about yourself.
- If you do not have a regular job, it is important to find other ways to work such as volunteer activities, hobbies, or whatever suits the person best.
- A homemaker should maintain strong feelings about the importance of her job because being a good wife and mother to me is the most important job a woman can have.
- Facial expressions are one of the most important body languages that we display.
- Inward beauty is one aspect that cannot be overlooked and radiates through our outward actions and speech.
- A lack of inward beauty can destroy the outward beauty.
- A wife with compassion and kindness for her family and others and truly gives of herself cannot help but be admired.

- Become very aware before it is too late what kind of influence you are having on your children. Each thing that you say or do in front of a child is education to him or her so it is important to be a good example.
- One area of beauty that becomes tarnished with our personalities is a critical spirit. It becomes a habit, so become aware of your speech pattern and begin to correct any criticism.
- Many people have a low self image because they could never quite live up to their parents expectations and it has affected the way they feel about themselves.
- Building a good self image in a child is so important and they build that self image by what is said to him or her.
- One of the most important areas that a family should work on is respect for each other and each others property.
- Demonstrate respect and love in a husband wife relationship by being kind, considerate, and sensitive to each others feelings and your children will learn from this.
- An example of a beautiful mother would be demonstrating respect for herself by caring for her personal needs as well as her household so that your children may develop these values.
- A beautiful woman will avoid bickering, nagging or criticizing.
- A beautiful woman will use gentle feminine persuasion or compromise.
- Beauty is a feeling of well being and feeling fulfilled in whatever sphere of life you have chosen.
- When you take time for yourself you will find that you will be better able to give of yourself to the people around you such as your family in a more positive way.
- A feeling of well being is taking control of your life and not relying on false stimuli or sedatives such as cigarettes, alcohol, sleeping pills and tranquilizers to prop you up.
- Learning to get our priorities in the right order is one of the first things that we need to do when starting to improve and take control of our lives.
- Learn to be flexible and roll with the tides.
- Organize your priorities around the things that matter to you and recognize what you want to achieve.
- We would all agree that what is on the inside of a person is the most important but we as individuals and a society put a premium on what we look like on the outside.
- We feel better about ourselves inside when we look the best we can on the outside.
- Energy is beauty and is needed to do the best in this world. It is not exciting to be around someone who is lacking enthusiasm or energy to do things.
- Physical energy not only comes from proper food and health care but springs from proper clothing and comfortable surroundings.
- If you wear clothes that are uncomfortable, it can affect your energy level as well as your mood. Do collars ride up on your neck? Are belts too snug and skirts or waistbands too tight? Are the shoes comfortable? All of these may be small points but they sap energy.
- Don't spread yourself too thin.
- Sit down and take a break and don't feel guilty about it.

- Learn to ignore those things that you cannot change. When life gets too much take it inch by inch.
- Create a special place in your home where you can renew your thoughts. It may be a comfortable rocking chair or the kitchen table, but take time to reflect on your life and get things into perspective.
- When I was growing up, even though I did not know how important it was to take time for myself, as a child I had a special place where I could observe the sky, watch the clouds and just dream by special dreams. It was up by an old railroad track that was close to my home and even today I love to go up there and walk by the tracks. It brings back all of the peaceful feelings.
- When you take this time to refresh yourself, you will find that you can give of yourself to your family and to the world with a whole new attitude.
- Take time for yourself and then you can give to other people in a more effective way.
- Develop a hobby which interests you.
- Begin to believe in yourself and act upon it. As you act on the basis of what you accept as true about yourself, you begin to believe that it is really true. You believed in yourself when you were small by believing that you could walk and talk.
- Doubts begin to come in when we do not live up to someone else's expectations or maybe because we failed at something that we tried.
- The way to replace self doubt with belief in yourself is to make it a habit to act as if you can do what you really want to do and keep saying to yourself that you can do it. Self confidence will then being to increase.
- One fact of life that always helps me is the fact that your and I have a great power and that is the power of choice. You can choose to make yourself miserable or happy just like you can choose to eat all you want, but if you do so is to give up your trim figure.
- When you create a positive image of yourself, it is important to keep a certain standard of dress and consistency of style.
- An aspiring person who is headed for the top should look like they are headed for the top.
- In the business world, do not leave people dangling. Sometimes we think if we ignore a problem, it will go away but it doesn't. This is good advice for bosses who are dealing with people in an office.
- It is important in the professional world to join and support your association that represents your profession.
- It is always pleasant to be around someone who makes you feel accepted and important to them, so accepting someone just the way they are, not that we all don't see improvement, but accepting that person is a special gift.
- Joy is the leavening in beauty but there are too many people that have pulled down corners of a tight mouth. This is not only unattractive but also aging.
- There is no more enchanting quality in this world that to be able to laugh at ones self.
- Being joyful can be captured by practicing the counting of our blessings and savoring our joys whether big or small.

- Simple pleasures and blessing that we often overlook can be a new idea we had for the day or relaxing with a friend
- Beauty needs organization of inner and outer self.
- Everyday with out fail, you must take time for yourself.
- It takes a firm determination not to waste time and emotion on what cannot be changed. This means people, jobs and the world.
- When you think of beauty, most people immediately think of outward beauty that is seen but there is a lot more to being an attractive person than that.
- Harmony in ones mind and soul is important to make someone pleasant.
- Feeling good about yourself and where you are going brings a feeling of harmony into your life.
- The outward expression to those around us certainly make a difference in whether we are attractive to that person or not.
- Be aware when you are really unhappy with yourself that you refrain from taking your bad feelings out on others.
- Your outer glow and your interest in others are all visible means of beauty and helps others to see you as a beautiful person.
- Many people have to work at having a loving personality. Do not be unkind to yourself by running yourself down and trying to find reasons why people should not like you.
- I cannot make myself feel inferior with out my consent.
- One important thing that makes us happy is doing things for others. Why not take time today to do something for someone else for no reason at all.
- Cook an imaginative dinner for someone.
- Bake goodies for someone and take it to them with a nice note telling them what they have meant to you.
- Fix extra dinner when you are cooking and freeze it and give it to a person who does not have much time or has been ill.
- Write frequent notes to people expressing your love and appreciation to them.
- Write a note sprinkled with his favorite perfume to your spouse and stick it in his lunch box, brief case, or leave it on his pillow.
- Perhaps you have a friend with a busy schedule or a lot of children and never has a chance for an evening alone with her husband. Volunteer to take the kids for a night so they can have a romantic meal in their home.
- I don't think there is anything that improves our image more than to be a loving and giving person.
- Learn to do at least one thing exceptionally well.
- Learn to focus on what you have done well and it will increase your confidence because there are enough people who will point our your shortcoming.
- Our doubting of ourselves begins when we didn't live up to someone's expectations of us or perhaps it began when we failed at something we tried.
- Make it a habit to constantly act as if the best things you want to believe about yourself are really true.

- Your self confidence will increase in direct proportion to the amount you have prepared yourself for a task.
- Many people have a hard time receiving complements but whether you are giving or receiving praise, a sincere compliment can be the first step toward friendship.
- The statistics show that people that have a good self image are able to accept compliments and praise much more gracefully than one who has grown up with feelings that they are not worth much.
- Let your imagination flow and do creative things all year long to make someone else happier and you will end up being a happier person.
- Our attitudes are a reflection of our inner feelings and is reflected in smiles, the way we greet someone, the way we talk on the phone and can make us appear either beautiful or unattractive to others.
- Our attitude is the way that we look at everyday life and gives us a beautiful or a sour spirit.
- We have a great power and that is the power of choice. We can choose to fret and stew, be inconsiderate and harsh or perhaps a better choice would be to relax and trust a higher and greater power than we have to take care of our worries and give us a spirit of peace and joy even in the midst of trials.
- You need to take breaks during the day to recharge your psyche. Everyone needs somewhere to surround themselves with a pleasant environment.
- Do not let the day go by without doing at least one thing that you really want to do whether it is watch something special on TV or take or walk, or read awhile. It is hard on ones personality when they do not have a chance to do one thing except what they had to do.
- Do simple little things that give pleasure like a flower in the bathroom, giving a gift, doing something special for you loved one.
- The power of touching cannot be underestimated. By touching someone, we can affirm our friendship and approval of them, communicate a positive message and promote health.
- Many people avoid the simple act of touching such as a pat on the back, handshakes, and cordial hugs which all affirm goodwill.
- Learn to be an effective touching person.
- The stress that is best for you is the one that will take you up to but not beyond your limits.
- Stress can be very productive giving you the drive to create, strive and achieve. It is too much stress that leads to tension and ill health. Balance is the key.
- Be discerning about what you fill your mind with. For instance, watching too many shows on TV that discuss problems and all the negatives of life can create more stress and anxiety in your own life.

THE ULTIMATE IMAGE

When we think of improving our image, we generally think of things to do on the outside to look better but one of the most important beauty improvements should be how we treat one another and what kind of attitude we reflect to others. One of the places that I would hope our images could improve would be with our families.

It is easy to let our hair down and take all of our frustrations out on them but they are the ones that we love the most and should get the best of us not only on the outside but inside also.

It is the place where we look the sloppiest with the least makeup and small petty annoyances get in the way of enjoying life.

Sometimes when we are unhappy with ourselves, it is very hard to keep from taking our bad feelings and tensions out on others.

Everyone has tensions and worries because there is no way to avoid them but it is not the problem but how you face it that counts. We have heard that said so often and it never seems to change anything but when you let God sit on the throne of your life and help you with all the frustrations of life, instead of trying to manipulate them yourself, something seems to happen to our attitude.

We can try and try to change ourselves inside but until we have a beautiful spirit with the Lord part of our everyday living, true beauty from within can be elusive.

Why not sit down today and have a good talk with the Lord and tell him how you feel about yourself and what you would like to change and be different and ask him to come into your heart and life and take over the mess you have made and ask his forgiveness for trying to do it yourself. If you sincerely do that, he will come in and help you become the person you desire to be.

We are not taken out of trials, temptations, or frustrations but God will help you through them and give you triumph over them. Easy to say and hard to do because we are so used to carrying our own burdens and having our own way that giving up completely in faith to God and letting Him have His way in our lives means control shifts from us to the Lord.

Sometimes a burden that I have over something is so hard to give to Him because I want it done my way and I am afraid God will not do what I want. What I have found however, is that when the crises or problem and worry were past and taken care of, if God would have answered the way that I prayed, things would have really been a mess but when I can look back and see how everything worked out God's way, it was so much better than how I had everything planned.

It continues to amaze me also how God can take such bad situations and when they are given to Him to solve and take care of, he makes a flower garden beyond our wildest imaginations.

Romans 8:28 says," All things work together for good to those that love the Lord and are called according to His purpose."

God has a plan for every life on this earth and somehow seeking and living in that plan brings us the happiness and peace we all seek.

Trying to live life out of God's plan eventually brings frustration and the inner beauty we so desire becomes tarnished from trying to be beautiful from within on our own power. What I am trying to say is trying to improve your image inside without allowing the peace of God to reign will be fruitless and the unsettled spirit within us will keep us from becoming the person God intended us to be.

When I look at the world we live in and the complexity of the creation, it humbles me to think that a God so omnipotent could care about me and my trials but He does. The intricate petals of a flower or even a dew drop are beyond my comprehension but when I focus on these magnificent creations, I know that a God that powerful can certainly take care of me and my purpose.